1979

ASPECTS OF LITERARY
THEORY AND PRACTICE
1550-1870

ASPECTS OF LITERARY THEORY AND PRACTICE

1550-1870

BY

P. G. THOMAS

KENNIKAT PRESS
Port Washington, N. Y./London

ASPECTS OF LITERARY THEORY AND PRACTICE

First published in 1931
Reissued in 1970 by Kennikat Press
Library of Congress Catalog Card No: 76-105841
ISBN 0-8046-0983-7

Manufactured by Taylor Publishing Company   Dallas, Texas

CONTENTS

CONTENTS

I

WHAT IS POETRY?

IT may be maintained that no branch of culture has been regarded with more general suspicion than the art of poetry. The achievements of science confront us hourly and compel admiration; painting serves, if nothing else, decorative purposes, while music possesses, at least, a tune. Yet many must have asked themselves : " Of what use is poetry ? "

It is to be feared that, despite explanations and definitions, poetry must in the long run justify its own existence, like the toucan. " How astonishing," wrote Sydney Smith in a review of Waterton's *Wanderings*, " are the freaks and fancies of nature ! To what purpose, we say, is a bird placed in the woods of Cayenne, with a bill a yard long, making a noise like a puppy-dog and laying eggs in hollow trees? To be sure, the toucan might retort : ' To what purpose were gentlemen in Bond Street created. . . . ? ' There is no end to such questions. So we will not venture into the metaphysics of the toucan." Nor is it necessary to venture into the metaphysics of poetry, beyond citing a few generalizations, proposed from time to time, to serve as signposts by the way.

Poetry has been defined as " the concrete and artistic expression of the human mind in emotional and rhythmical language " (Watts-Dunton). The definition, while recognizing that poetic art has both a sensuous and a technical aspect, suggests, at the same time, their independence. Yet it is only by a process

9

of abstraction that emotion and technique can be considered separable elements in verse. A famous definition of Wordsworth's describes poetry as " the image of man and nature. . . . The spontaneous overflow of powerful feelings, it takes its origin from emotion recollected in tranquillity "—but, apart from the stress laid on the function of memory, this definition covers the rest of the fine arts. In the *Biographia Literaria*, Coleridge asserted that a poem is " discriminated by proposing to itself such delight from the whole as is compatible with a distinct gratification from each component part." This is helpful in that it enables us to exclude from the category of poetry mere rhymed doggerel, such as mnemonics for recalling the days of the month :

> Thirty days hath September,
> April, June and November,

or alphabetic rhymes :

> An Austrian army awfully arrayed
> Boldly by batteries besieged Belgrade,

or versified statements of mere fact :

> I put my hat upon my head
> And went into the Strand,
> And there I met another man
> Whose hat was in his hand.

But wit is not thereby excluded, though necessarily occupying a niche apart. A happy example in this vein occurs in Praed's *King of the Sandwich Islands*, in which the poet indirectly satirizes contemporary politics :

> The people in his happy reign
> Were blest beyond all other nations:
> Unharmed by foreign axe and chain,
> Unhealed by civic innovations;
> They served the usual logs and stones,
> With all the usual rites and terrors,
> And swallowed all their father's bones,
> And swallowed all their father's errors.

> When the fierce mob, with clubs and knives,
>   All swore that nothing should prevent them,
> But that their representatives
>   Should actually represent them,
> He interposed the proper checks,
>   By sending troops with drums and banners,
> To cut their *speeches* short, and necks,
>   And break their heads to mend their manners.

To the modern mind the conception of poetry is closely knit up with the traditional ideas, *romantic* and *romanticism*. Mere tentative suggestions as to the content of these terms must needs serve in *lieu* of definition. The romantic method is the liberal, free, ramifying method of Shakespeare and of Wordsworth. In the spirit of romance the medieval poet cited Plato over against St. Paul, the Sybil side by side with David :

> Teste David cum Sibylla.

In the same spirit the Elizabethan bohemian penned his sonnet to Celia's eyebrow, or laboured out a *cento* of verses in honour of Gloriana. But the full tide of romance was delayed till the French Revolution, when alien forces from the Celtic borderland, from Greece and the Middle Ages, concentrated in England. Romanticism, in its fullest conception, is no more realized by Keats, with his vision of " casements opening on the foam of perilous seas in faery lands forlorn," than by Landor, designing imaginary conversations between the masters of letters in bygone ages, or Macpherson, collector of legends of the Celtic prime, or Walpole, designer of a Gothic mansion and a Gothic romance. Yet all display distinctly romantic aspects, combined, on occasion, with a sense of form as distinctly classical. The cruder types of romance, fashionable towards the end of the eighteenth century, were affectionately parodied by Crabbe in the *Library*, a passage from which may serve to recall a bygone mode :

> Hence, ye profane! I feel a former dread,
> A thousand visions float around my head;

> Hark! hollow blasts through empty courts resound,
> And shadowy forms with staring eyes stalk round;
> See! moats and bridges, walls and castles rise,
> Ghosts, fairies, demons, dance before our eyes;
> Lo! magic verse inscribed on golden gate,
> And bloody hand that beckons on to fate:
> "And who art thou, thou little page, unfold?
> Say, doth thy lord my Claribel withhold?
> Go, tell him straight, Sir Knight, thou must resign
> The captive queen; for Claribel is mine."
> Away he flies; and now for bloody deeds,
> Black suits of armour, masks and foaming steeds;
> The giant falls; his recreant throat I seize,
> And from his corslet take the massy keys:
> Dukes, lords and knights, in long procession move,
> Released from bondage with my virgin love:
> She comes! she comes! in all the charms of youth,
> Unequalled love and unexpected truth!

But poetry, an organ of many stops, responded readily to the touch of each new performer, and rapidly advanced beyond mere crudities. Novel experiments in metre on models, French and Italian, supplied new interpretative mediums, responsive to every mood of the soul. In Byron's *Prophecy of Dante* poetry became prophetic and the exile of Ravenna a guide to future ages:

> The age which I anticipate, no less
> Shall be the Age of Beauty, and while whelms
> Calamity the nations with distress,
> The genius of my country shall arise,
> A cedar towering in the wilderness.

Thus poetry came to resemble a remoter way of thinking, an effort to express at least one aspect of the poet's ideal.

Turning to other influences—the foundation of the Royal Academy and the plundering of the Parthenon, which dazzled the world with the wonder of ancient art and sculpture, produced in poetry allied effects, and established a kinship between the arts. The new Hellenism, which had received sanction in the bringing over of the Elgin marbles in 1816, took captive Keats and Landor, and realized its greatest product in

Prometheus Unbound. While Keats continued to dedicate festal hymns to Apollo and the god Pan,

> Whose mighty palace roof doth hang
> From jagged trunks, and overshadoweth
> Eternal whispers,

while Landor renewed the cult of the Grecian deities, Shelley was engaged in a literary study of Æschylus and in speculations as to the fate of the fire-giver. The dying gladiator in Byron's poem has the cold touch of the sculptor, and points to kindred influences. ¡The Hellenistic movement was, in fact, mainly responsible for the recovery of this classic sense of form.

Meantime, effects of painting, derived from Italy, predominated in Keats, combined with subtle movements, purely poetical. This pictorial power, aided by suggestions of contrast, is seen at its height in the *Eve of St. Agnes*, a series of visions composed in Spenserian stanzas and shot with imaginative colouring :

> A casement high and triple-arch'd there was,
> All garlanded with carven imag'ries
> Of fruits and flowers, and bunches of knot-grass,
> And diamonded with panes of quaint device,
> Innumerable of stains and splendid dyes,
> As are the tiger-moth's deep damask'd wings;
> And in the midst, 'mong thousand heraldries,
> And twilight saints, and dim emblazonings,
> A shielded scutcheon blush'd with blood of queens and kings.

Writing in 1821, Hazlitt declared he regretted he was not young enough to enter with full enjoyment into Keats's poem : " The beautiful and tender images there conjured up ' come like shadows—so depart.' The tiger-moth's wings which he has spread over his rich poetic blazonry just flit across my fancy; the gorgeous twilight window, which he has painted over again in his verse, to me ' blushes ' almost in vain ' with blood of queens and kings.' I know how I should have felt at one time in reading such passages."

This pictorial method Keats handed on to Tennyson,

who employed it with new effect in his account of
Lancelot's ride in the *Lady of Shalott* :

> A bow-shot from her bower-eaves,
> He rode between the barley-sheaves,
> The sun came dazzling through the leaves,
> And flamed upon the brazen greaves
>   Of bold Sir Lancelot.
> A red-cross knight for ever kneel'd
> To a lady in his shield,
> That sparkled on the yellow field,
>   Beside remote Shalott.
>
> The gemmy bridle glitter'd free,
> Like to some branch of stars we see
> Hung in the golden Galaxy.
> The bridle bells rang merrily
>   As he rode down to Camelot:
> And from his blazon'd baldric slung
> A mighty silver bugle hung,
> And as he rode his armour rung
>   Beside remote Shalott.

That this is more than mere painting is proved by the
employment of the simile and other features.   A painter
would have been hard put to it to get in the comparison
with the " branch of stars."

Meantime, the simpler effects of romanticism—
interest in nature and in man—had ceased to carry
novelty, and natural scenery underwent a transforma-
tion in the minds of Coleridge and Wordsworth.   The
ghostly terrors that involve the person of the ancient
mariner,

> I fear thee and thy glittering eye
> And thy skinny hand so brown,
> Fear not, fear not, thou Wedding Guest,
> This body dropped not down,

are elements in a new and supernatural view of the
universe, which, in Shelley, resemble the hauntings of
a spirit-world.

Shelley conceived the poet as a product of countless
unseen forces :

> He will watch from dawn to gloom
> The lake-reflected sun illume
> The yellow bees in the ivy-bloom,
> Nor heed nor see what things they be;
> But from these create he can
> Forms more real than living man,
> Nurslings of Immortality,

but, as Francis Thompson put it : " This is the child's faculty of make-believe raised to the nth power. He is still at play, save only that his play is such as manhood stops to watch, and his playthings are those which the gods give their children. The universe is his box of toys. He dabbles his fingers in the dayfall. He is gold-dusty with tumbling amidst the stars."

For a modern equivalent one turns to Arthur O'Shaughnessy's *Music and Moonlight*, also concerned with the poet's function :

> We are the music-makers
> And we are the dreamers of dreams,
> Wandering by lone sea-breakers,
> And sitting by desolate streams;
> World-losers and world-forsakers,
> On whom the pale moon gleams;
> For we are the movers and shakers
> Of the world for ever, it seems.

As for the relationship between poetry and the fine arts generally, rhythm plays an important part in the former, and rhythm is allied to music. The difference is a difference of instrument. It belongs to prosody to illustrate the countless subtle devices, whereby a skilful metrist varies his lines. Any of the great passages in Milton will repay study a hundredfold—a song from *Comus*, a passage from *Paradise Lost*, or a chorus from *Samson Agonistes* :

> All is best, though we oft doubt
> What the unsearchable dispose
> Of Highest Wisdom brings about,
> And ever best found in the close.
> Oft he seems to hide his face,
> But unexpectedly returns

> And to his faithful champion hath in place
> Bore witness gloriously; whence Gaza mourns,
> And all that band them to resist
> His uncontrollable intent.
> His servants he with new acquist
> Of true experience from this great event,
> With peace and consolation hath dismissed,
> And calm of mind, all passion spent.

The bold displacing of the accent, the shifting of the pause, the device of repetition, the use of overlapped lines—these are mere technicalities to cover the least subtle of the poet's devices. Originally, the whole matter depends upon the right choice of words. " Beautiful words," said Longinus, " are in deed and in fact the very light of the spirit," and Pater speaks of the æsthetic satisfaction to be found " in that frugal closeness of style which makes the most of a word, in the exaction from every sentence of a precise relief, in the just spacing out of word to thought, in the logically filled space, connected always with the delightful sense of difficulty overcome." Yet, as a cathedral admits of gargoyles in its architectural scheme, so in poetry is there room for the grotesque. Browning's *Ring and the Book*, despite amazing felicities, abounds in crudities, jolts, harshness, and even coarseness, and his *Holy-Cross Day* is a sovereign example in this manner :

> Fee, faw, fum ! bubble and squeak !
> Blessedest Thursday's the fat of the week.
> Rumble and tumble, sleek and rough,
> Stinking and savoury, smug and gruff,
> Take the church-road, for the bell's due chime
> Gives us the summons—'tis sermon-time !

But this is the method of the strong, to be eschewed by the weak. It is by a mysterious concatenation of vowel and consonant that the melodious effect of poetry is produced, which effect may be adapted to various ends. Direct imitations of nature, as in the Tennysonian

> Low on the sand, and loud on the stone,
> The last wheel echoes away,

or Browning's

> There was a rustling that seemed like a bustling
> Of merry crowds justling at pitching and hustling;
> Small feet were pattering, wooden shoes clattering,
> Little hands clapping and little tongues chattering,

—these may be classed among the recreations of the poet. But, where sound is made subservient to sense, the highest artistic effect is achieved.

In that exquisitely modulated address of the Emperor Hadrian to his soul the carefully selected and endearing diminutives compel sympathy, despite the veil of a more or less unfamiliar tongue. To the poet's affection, the soul becomes, in turn, a little wandering thing, an alluring, a pale, a little naked thing, or, as Byron rendered it :

> A gentle, fleeting, wavering sprite,
> Friend and associate of the clay.

The original actually runs :

> Animula, vagula, blandula
> Hospes, comesque corporis,
> Quae nunc abibis in loca?
> Pallidula, rigida, nudula.

Again, the pleasure derived from the great choric song in the *Lotos-Eaters* is, by no means, limited to a sense of its dream-music; one is throughout haunted by an idea—that of the fatal plant which holds captive Ulysses and his crew. Of the riotous passion for pure sound there is more in Swinburne, where every device of metrical skill has been enlisted in the service of art. In those stanzas, in which the sweetest of the sounds of earth and heaven are weighed and reckoned as naught beside the melody of a " child's clear laughter," the interweaving of sound and sense finds perfect illustration :

> Golden bells of welcome rolled
> Never forth such notes, nor told
> Hours so blithe in tones so bold,
> As the radiant mouth of gold
> Here that rings forth heaven.

> If the golden-crested wren
> Were a nightingale—why, then,
> Something seen and heard by men
> Might be half as sweet as when
> Laughs a child of seven.

Imagery is no less striking a feature of style, and, here, poetry allies itself with painting. The effect is not entirely dependent upon accuracy of outline and attention to detail, so that the poet's method constantly varies. The strength of the so-called classical, as opposed to the romantic, method lay precisely in its rejection of the commonplace and its adherence to broad outline, whereby the general effect might be the more readily grasped. This method—in its widest sense— finds illustration in Matthew Arnold's *Sohrab and Rustum*:

> So on the bloody sand Sohrab lay dead,
> And the great Rustum drew his horseman's cloak
> Down o'er his face, and sate by his dead son.
> As those black granite pillars, once high reared
> By Jemshid in Persepolis to bear
> His house, now, mid their broken flights of steps
> Lie prone, enormous, down the mountain side,
> So in the sand lay Rustum by his son.

Through neglect of such principles, Wordsworth, in his description of Simon Lee, leaves the impression that he is handling a mere bundle of sticks, while Goldsmith's woodcut in the *Traveller* might well have served for a description of the tiers of benches in a theatre:

> And he is lean and he is sick;
> His body, dwindled and awry,
> Rests upon ankles swoln and thick;
> His legs are thin and dry.
> One prop he has, and only one,
> His wife, an aged woman,
> Lives with him, near the waterfall,
> Upon the village Common.

The huntsman's legs, then, are props, and his wife merely the chief of these, the ludicrous effect produced being hardly that intended.

It is in suggestion, then, that the safest resource of
the artist lies. A single stroke of the pen, in alliance
with the forces of the imagination, is often more effective
than a wealth of descriptive detail. In any landscape,
again, the scene tends to be transfused and coloured
by the artist's personality. Certain scenes and localities
linger in the memory under particular aspects, and bear
the impress of particular minds. In this way, Shelley's
landscapes appear shot with the ethereal tint of his
imagination, while the luxurious sensuousness of Keats
leaves an impress of another tone.

Of Shelley's nature-method the following is typical :

> Under the bowers
> Where the Ocean powers
> Sit on their pearlèd thrones;
> Through the coral woods
> Of the weltering floods
> Over heaps of unvalued stones;
> Through the dim beams
> Which amid the streams
> Weave a network of coloured light;
> And under the caves
> Where the shadowy waves
> Are as green as the forest's night.

As for Byron, the stanzas of *Childe Harold* are almost
invariably touched with the bravado and pose character-
istic of that poet :

> The moon is up; by Heaven a lovely eve,

and so on. But Wordsworth's nature-sketches are rarely
far from the sublime. Illustrations abound, though one
thinks first of the sonnet composed on the beach near
Calais, of the lines to Lucy, or the exquisite *Green
Linnet:*

> My dazzled sight he oft deceives,
> A brother of the dancing leaves;
> Then flits, and from the cottage eaves
> Pours forth his song in gushes;
> As if by that exulting strain
> He mocked and treated with disdain
> The voiceless form he chose to feign,
> While fluttering in the bushes.

Here the poet attains the ends of his art by conceiving nature and humanity as an aspect of the infinite—*sub specie æternitatis*. He provides us, as Professor Moore-Smith says, with " hours of escape from the smallness of our surroundings into a wider and fairer world where our senses are charmed, our emotions stimulated, and our thoughts raised; and then, when we have returned from those spiritual travels to the old routine and the old dull scenes, he irradiates those scenes for us with something of the light that never was on sea or land."

An analogy between poetry and sculpture is also traceable, since there is less of pictorial quality in clear cut, restrained, marble-like verse, where accuracy of workmanship, symmetry, and expression are the dominant characteristics. Here there is little place for colour, but more for the development of form, as in Matthew Arnold's portrait of Circe in the *Strayed Reveller*:

> Thou standest, smiling
> Down on me; thy right arm,
> Lean'd up against the column there,
> Props thy soft cheek;
> Thy left holds, hanging loosely,
> The deep cup, ivy-cinctur'd,
> I held but now.

Collins's odes have this cold touch, while Keats, in his *Grecian Urn*, seems to have caught his lover in sculpturesque outline as he bends over the form of his mistress:

> For ever wilt thou love and she be fair.

Here, on the formal side, the classic school is pre-eminent. The great types—the ode, the epic, the elegy —were carved out by classic poets with supreme constructive ability, and if romanticism can claim as its own the sonnet, the Spenserian stanza, and a score of forms, laboured out by *jongleur* and *trouvère* and troubadour, it must be admitted that these are handled,

as a rule, with less structural skill and architectonic
insight. For types of perfect artistic construction one
looks to poems conceived in the spirit of Landor's *Rose
Aylmer* or Edgar Allan Poe's *Helen*, with its half-
Greek, half-romantic reference to those

> Nicean barks of yore,
> That gently o'er a perfumed sea,
> The weary wayworn traveller bore
> To his own native shore.

Only upon analysis does the structure of such work
become apparent. In the drama the architectonic
element lies upon the surface, but in no poetic type is
it non-existent. Watts-Dunton has said, for example,
of Tennyson's *Palace of Art*, that " the whole edifice,
as described, rises as lightly as a lyric; it is full of the
surge of the hunger for beauty, and yet a man might
almost build upon the description as upon plans of an
architect " :

> Four courts I made, East, West and South, and North,
> In each a squared lawn wherefrom
> The golden gorge of dragons spouted forth
> A flood of fountain-foam.
>
> And round the cool green courts there ran a row
> Of cloisters, branched with mighty woods,
> Echoing all night to that sonorous flow
> Of spouted fountain-floods.
>
> And round the roofs a gilded gallery
> That leant broad verge to distant lands,
> Far as the wild swan wings, to where the sky
> Dipt down to sea and sands.

In a poem like the *Excursion* the artistic foundations
are apparent, and tend to reveal " the solid strength of
the structure," the weight of the lines depending upon
a mighty iambic movement, an alternation of short and
long syllables. The same constructive power is implicit
in Dante's conception of the *Inferno* and in the *Paradise*
of Milton, where the use of rule and square is through-
out apparent. On the other hand, the forces control-
ling the design of the *Castle of Indolence* are different :

the structure rises like a dream and is as evanescent—
ready to be carried away at a breath. So, with the
Ode to the West Wind, where, as Watts-Dunton says,
the artistic methods " contradict the idea of solid
strength," and, by their employment of anapæstic and
dactylic measures, " make the structure appear to hang
over our heads like the cloud pageantry of heaven."
In this way, the methods of the two schools tend to
interweave.

But poetry, while it unites in itself qualities of form,
order, melody, and colour, is of itself none of these
things. They are but the accessories, which the poet
welds together under the force of his imagination. They
furnish principles, according to which he arranges and
co-ordinates his matter. The real appeal is to the
intellect, since it is with a word as instrument that the
poet works, and words convey meaning. As Dr.
Bridges well expressed it : " The other fine arts aim
also at spiritual expression, but their material forms
are more remote from ideas, and their interpretation
often requires some special disposition of mind. But
in poetry the material is language, and words are not
only familiar to all of us but are of all forms the most
significant that we have." The very antiquity of speech
imparts to it a suggestive power, which serves to lead
the mind to things of olden time. The mere names of
romance raise an emotion unachieved by any modern
equivalent, and possess a fascination for all who have
lingered over tales

> Of fairy damsels met in forest wide,
> By knight of Logres or of Lyones,
> Lancelot, or Pelleas, or Pellenore.

Here, in suggestion, the greatest function of language
lies. The amateur poet may perfect his rhyme, obtain
the fit image, secure a just architectural effect, equip
himself with " taffeta phrases " and " silken terms
precise," yet, of itself, this cannot make literature. The
joys and sorrows of the heart, hope and despair, life

and death—these things refuse to be confined within the pages of a book. Herein lies the explanation of the grand style. To confuse the methods of the arts, to draw effects of picture out of rhythm, to cause architectural structure to melt into harmony—this is the manner of Shakespeare and the romantics. By subordinating nature to the soul of man, the great men-of-letters of every age have become interpreters of life and promoters of morality. In one sublime conception Dante summed up the whole of medieval theology, bequeathing to later generations its vital thought and signification. That incomparable line from the *Commedia,*

e la sua volontate è nostra pace,

owes its acceptance as much to its high seriousness as to its literary quality. It constitutes, indeed, a supreme example of that grand style, of which Matthew Arnold collected examples to serve as touchstones for the recognition of great literature. Here belong Simonides' lines on the Lacedæmonians who fell at Thermophylæ :

Strangers, bear this message to the Spartans,
That we lie here obedient to their laws,

likewise Milton's

But his face
Deep scars of thunder had intrench'd and care
Sat on his faded cheek,

besides many Shakespearian passages.

But the method, by which the things of time and space may be subordinated to a lofty ethic purpose, finds illustration everywhere throughout the poets. There is, for example, Blake's *War Song to Englishmen,* or his lines from *Milton,* Wordsworth's *Tintern Abbey,* or that passage in the *Vision of Sin,* in which Tennyson identifies the quietude of nature with God Himself :

I saw that every morning, far withdrawn
Beyond the darkness and the cataract,
God made Himself an awful rose of dawn,
Unheeded: and detaching, fold by fold,
From those still heights, and, slowly drawing near,
A vapour heavy, hueless, formless, cold,
Came floating on for many a month and year,
Unheeded: and I thought I would have spoken,
And warn'd that madman ere it grew too late:
But, as in dreams, I could not.

It is this many-sidedness of poetry, allied with its sovereign appeal to the intellect through the medium of language, that assures its high position among educative instruments, and makes it conceivable that the vital part of our thought to-day is its unconscious poetry.

As for the poet himself, his task will always remain one of supreme difficulty since, in the words of an ancient critic: " Nature without art is insufficient to anyone for achievement, likewise art without nature. . . . It is natural gift, goodwill, patience, method that make a good and wise poet. Number of years makes neither, but merely makes him old " (Simylus).

II

THE FOUNDATIONS OF CRITICISM

IN all literatures criticism is an after-growth, and it was subsequent to the bloom and decay of Elizabethan drama that scientific criticism made its appearance in seventeenth century England. Elizabethan criticism had been largely tentative and stimulated by controversy. Its main themes—the antiquity of poetry, its nature, and purpose—formed the staple of Sidney's *Apology* (1583). At the same time, discussion centred in the special problems of *decorum*, *prosody*, and *diction*—concerning which variety of opinion existed within the critical camp. As employed by Sidney, *decorum* was equivalent to propriety, hence *Gorbuduc* won his approval, whereas the romantic comedies offended him. Gascoigne adopted a similar standpoint, and was followed by Whetstone, whose remarks in *Promos and Cassandra* (1578) constitute a remarkable anticipation of Sidney. The romantic dramatist " first grounds his work on impossibilities, then in three hours runs through the world, marries, gets children, makes children men, men to conquer kingdoms, murder monsters, and brings God from Heaven and devils from hell." As regards *diction*, there was a general outcry against " ink-horn terms," excessive alliteration, and the over-florid in style. In his *Art of Rhetoric* (1553) Wilson set his face against French-English, English-Italianate, and Chaucerisms, while Ascham and Sidney concentrated on Euphuism. That most Elizabethan critics went astray on the subject of *prosody* is well-known, the experiments of Sidney, Spenser, and Webbe

25

surviving to prove the futility of the classical heresy. Campion's triumph in trochaics is merely the exception which proves the rule:

> Rose-cheekt Laura, come,
> Sing thou smoothly with thy beauty's
> Silent music, either other
> Sweetly gracing.
>
> Lovely forms do flow
> From consent divinely framed:
> Heaven is music and thy beauty's
> Birth is heavenly.

But the period produced a sane prosodic handbook in Gascoigne's *Notes of Instruction* (1575) and a remarkable *tour de force*, the *Defence of Rhyme* (c. 1603), in which Daniel, taking his stand upon custom and nature, raised his banner in defence of the moderns: " Methinks we should not so soon yield our consents captive to the authority of antiquity, unless we saw more reason; all our understandings are not to be built by the square of Greece and Italy. We are the children of nature as well as they."

The close of Elizabethan criticism was signalled by the appearance of Ben Jonson's *Discoveries* (c. 1621), concerning which Swinburne wrote : " None who have studied it can fail to recognize that its author was in every way worthy to have been the friend of Bacon and of Shakespeare." Doubtless, the two most considerable Elizabethan critics were Sidney and Jonson, of whom Sidney, who came first chronologically, must be reckoned with in the *Discoveries*. It was he who was mainly responsible for the Aristotelian influence in Elizabethan literature. The *Poetics*, practically without influence in Europe during the Middle Ages, had been retranslated into Latin in 1498 and into Italian in 1549, and by the revived Aristotelian canons the æsthetic bases of poetry were established. The link between Sidney and Aristotle is apparent in their regard for the doctrine of " imitation " or *mimesis*, but many elements in the *Apology* are traceable to Italian critics of the

cinquecento. Sidney followed Daniello and Minturno
in his recognition of prose-poetry—a heresy likely to be
perennial as long as prose like *Isaiah, Holy Dying,* and
Modern Painters continues to be written—and Italian
remained the chief critical influence during the Eliza-
bethan period. The stress laid by Sidney on the
abstract qualities of poetry, which, with Aristotle, he
considered *philosophoteron kai spoudaioteron,* that is,
more philosophical and studiously serious than history,
influenced Bacon, who accorded to the imagination the
special function of transforming " what has happened "
into " what may or should happen." In a famous
passage of the *Advancement,* Bacon wrote : " So as
it appeareth that poesy serveth and conferreth to
magnanimity, morality and to delectation. And there-
fore it was ever thougnt to have some participation of
divineness, because it doth raise and erect the mind, by
submitting the shows of things to the desires of the
mind; whereas reason doth buckle and bow the mind
unto the nature of things." Bacon has, indeed, been
claimed as the founder of literary history on the ground
of the following passage : " But a just story of learn-
ing, containing the antiquities and originals of know-
ledges and their sects, their inventions, their traditions,
their diverse administrations and managings, their
flourishings, their oppositions, decays, depressions,
oblivions, removes, with the causes and occasions of
them, and all other events concerning learning through-
out the ages of the world, *I may truly affirm to be
wanting* " (*Advancement,* Book II).

Ben Jonson's *Discoveries* forms a link between
sixteenth and seventeenth century criticism. This little
treatise, described by its author as a series of aphorisms
" made upon men and matter, as they have flowed out
of his daily readings," is characterized by acumen and
a fine gift of style. It has been conjectured that the
dicta of the *Discoveries* were merely " the fragments,
disunited and disjointed, of single and continuous

essays on various great subjects." Thus, the nucleus of an essay on style appears side by side with slighter remarks on literary history (Marlowe, Bacon, Shakespeare), the morality of letters, and the fine arts in general. The investigations of Mr. Schelling have further proved that many passages were direct imitations, or even quotations, of passages which Jonson came across in his daily reading. A remark so apparently intimate as the following : " I have known a man vehement on both sides, that knew no mean, either to intermit his studies or call upon them again," turns out to be a translation from the elder Seneca, while the lines on *amor patriæ* : " There is a necessity all men should love their country : he that professeth the contrary may be delighted with his words, but his heart is there," derive from Euripides. Even the famous *sufflaminandus erat* passage is traceable to the elder Seneca.

For much of his matter Jonson was, thus, under obligation—to Quintilian or Aristotle, to Pontanus or Heinsius—and the verdict of Dryden is confirmed : " You track him everywhere in their snow." Stress must be laid upon the debt to Heinsius, since this explains the position occupied by Jonson as a forerunner of classical criticism. In the pages of the Dutch critic it was possible to find the Aristotelian position clearly expressed without undue slavishness; his treatise supplied an authoritative handbook for the neo-classical school. Under such influences, Jonson devoted his attention, more and more, to technique, and largely deserted the freer standpoint of Sidney.

The first half of the seventeenth century supplied several curious examples of the different directions, in which critics were impelled. Bolton in his *Hypercritica* (1618), Peacham in his *Complete Gentleman* (1622), Drayton in the *Epistle to Henry Reynolds* (1627), and Suckling in the *Session of the Poets* (1637) were content for the most part with scattered *dicta* on

predecessors or contemporaries. But in Reynolds'
Mythomystes (1633) the taste for metaphysics is curiously
exemplified, and poetry becomes something sacred and
divine. A saner book, though of no great importance
except as it serves to illustrate the growing taste for
reading, was Sir William Alexander's *Anacrisis*
(*c.* 1634), with its affectionate tributes to Virgil,
Heliodorus, Tasso, and Sidney. " It were enough to
be excellent by being second to Sidney, since whoever
could be that, behoved to be before others," remarked
Sir William, and his enthusiasm for both English and
foreign authors had some share in the establishment of
that comparative view of criticism, apart from which
progress would have been well-nigh impossible.

It was, as Spingarn has shown, the influence of
Hobbes, which as much as anything gave a new direc-
tion to criticism. The first to attempt a scientific analysis
of mental phenomena, Hobbes applied his results to
literary criticism. In his reply to Davenant's Preface
to *Gondibert* he gave the following analysis of the
mental faculties: " Time and education begets
experience; experience begets memory; memory begets
judgment and fancy; judgment begets the strength and
structure, and fancy begets the ornament of a poem."
This is obviously the standpoint of the materialist, and
was handed on to Hobbes's successors of the Restora-
tion, while his distinction between " judgment " and
" fancy " survived into the eighteenth century. Locke
substituted the term " wit " for " fancy," and, in a
passage quoted approvingly by Addison, declared that
wit lies " most in the assemblage of ideas and putting
those together with quickness and variety, wherein can
be found any resemblance or congruity, thereby to
make up pleasant pictures and agreeable visions in the
fancy; judgment, on the contrary, lies quite on the other
side, in separating carefully, one from another, ideas
wherein can be found the least difference, thereby to
avoid being misled by similitude and by affinity to

take one thing for another." Addison, however, added to Locke's definition : " It is necessary that the ideas should not lie too near one another in the nature of things," thus approximating to the modern differentiation. But wit is not identical with humour, as the romantics discovered, since, to quote Hazlitt, " humour is the describing the ludicrous as it is in itself; wit is the exposing it, by comparing it or contrasting it with something else. Humour is, as it were, the growth of nature and accident; wit is the product of art and fancy. Wit, as distinguished from poetry, is the imagination or fancy inverted, and so applied to given objects as to make the little look less, the mean more light and worthless; or to divert our admiration or wean our affections from that which is lofty and impressive, instead of producing a more intense admiration and exalted passion, as poetry does." Still, there is no stereotyped form of the definition, which varies from age to age, Dryden defining wit as " a propriety of thoughts and words," with which Pope's well-known " what oft was thought, but ne'er so well-expressed " falls into line.

The stress laid by Hobbes upon " judgment " gave the critic a recognized position in literature. The kinds of poetry were now clearly differentiated, and their provenance determined. According to Hobbes, poetry is classifiable as (1) epic, (2) tragic, (3) pastoral, (4) pastoral comic, (5) satire, and (6) comic, the kinds being thus kept rigorously apart. But the temper of the new criticism was only partly conditioned by developments in philosophy. Stress must be laid on the more thorough-going study of Aristotle, contact with French literature, represented in England by Saint Évremond and, abroad, by Corneille, together with the social forces, dominant under the Stuarts.

French criticism of the Renaissance period had opened with a trumpet-call in Du Bellay's *Défense et illustration de la langue française* (1549)—a summons to reinforce native literature with material from the classics. Abandoning the rondeaux, ballades, vire-layes, and other *épiceries* of the older school, Du Bellay had recourse to alien models—odes, elegies, and sonnets —of which he counselled " imitation." The terms, in which this is expressed, recall Vida—" Ly donques, et rely premierement (Ô Poete futur), fueillete, de main nocturne et journelle, les exemplaires Grecz et Latins " —yet Du Bellay was never as servilely classical as his predecessor. His aim, like that of his *côterie*, was to assist the natural aptitude of French poets by the creation of a new poetic diction. If he failed to appreciate the heritage of the earlier period, he at least formulated the manifesto of a school, capable of produc-ing the *Hélène* and *Cassandre* of Ronsard, Belleau's *Avril*, together with his own *Regrets*. How far Du Bellay was indebted to the Italians, Vida and Trissino, is not clear : he was, however, anticipated by Sibilet in his admiration for ode, elegy, and sonnet, even though this last had held no brief for " aureate " diction. The Pléiade reforms were not accepted without protest, though, on the whole, the opposition was weak. Pelletier was among the first to support the movement in his *Art Poétique* (1555), adopting that lofty view of the poet's function which Minturno had counten-anced. Ronsard expressed similar views in his *Abrégé* (1565) and in the prefaces to the *Franciade*, but is more interesting, when he turns aside to defend the " lexicon des vieils mots d'Artus, de Lancelot, et de Gauwain." It is to his credit that he restored to the French language many obsolete native words, and if, in contrast to this, he counselled classical innovation and the use of periphrasis, this was but natural in view of his efforts to strengthen the language. Ronsard's loyalty to his native tongue is, in any case, beyond dispute :

Je te conseille d'apprendre diligemment la langue Grecque et Latine, voir Italienne et Espagnole, puis, quand tu les sçauras

parfaitement, te retirer en ton enseigne comme un bon soldat et
composer en ta langue maternelle comme a fait Homère. . . .

The close of the first period was signalled by the
appearance of Vauquelin de la Fresnaye's *Art Poétique*
(1575-1605), in which are apparent the combined
influences of Aristotle and Horace, Vida and Minturno,
with the result that most of the critical doctrines of the
Renaissance are there summed up.

While the Pléiade revolt may be regarded as the
work of a *côterie* headed by Ronsard, a single individual
made himself responsible for the counter-revolution.
No doubt, reform was in the air and had the approval
of the *salons*; but Malherbe stood, for a time, alone,
enforcing his doctrines, both in theory and practice. In
many respects, the new movement was closely related
to its predecessor, but Malherbe went far in his reform
of diction and versification, and exposed himself to
Regnier's satire :

> Cependant leur scavoir ne s'estend seulement
> Qu'à regratter un mot douteux au jugement;
> Prendre garde qu'un qui ne heurte une diphtongue;
> Espier si des vers la rime est brève ou longue.

Yet, despite his lack of poetic sensibility, Malherbe
ranks as the founder of that classical French school,
which stood unopposed till well-nigh the close of the
eighteenth century. After him, French criticism
advanced apace, producing a bead-roll of writers,
comparable with that of the Italian *cinquecento*.

The preliminaries of critical organization fell, after
Malherbe, to Deimier and Ogier, with Chapelain,
Balzac, Vaugelas, and Racan in their wake. All adopted
a new standpoint inasmuch as, for them, poetry ceased
to be something sacred and sank into mere diversion :
" C'étoit sottise de faire des vers pour en esperer
autre récompence que son divertissement " (Racan : *Vie
de Malherbe*). The object of the poet is to give pleasure
and, later, to correct, for, as Malherbe put it baldly,
" un bon poète n'étoit pas plus utile a l'État qu'un bon

joueur de quilles." Poetic diction is to be eschewed, poetry being little more than measured prose, though marked by clarity and sobriety. In this spirit Malherbe pencilled the poems of Desportes, condemning expressions as plebeian, obsolete, pleonastic, or even foolish, and often denouncing the rhymes.

Meantime, attention was being given to dramatic theory, as expounded by Aristotle and interpreted by Scaliger, Castelvetro, and Heinsius. The neo-classic French school maintained that the aim of the theatre is the *purgation of the passions*, and that poetry must please by its conformity to the " rules," among them that of the " unities." Verisimilitude, again, was declared to be more important than truth :

Il n'y a . . . que le *Vraisemblable* qui puisse raisonnablement fonder, soûtenir et terminer un poëme dramatique; ce n'est pas que les choses véritables et possibles soient bannies du théâtre; mais elles n'y sont reçues qu'en tant qu'elles ont de la vraisemblance (D'Aubignac: *Pratique du théâtre*).

It was Corneille, who, in his various *Épitres* (1630-63), his *Trois Discours* (1660), and *Examens* (1660) ventured to challenge these restrictions. If the aim of the theatre be *katharsis*, the " purgation of the passions," he declares himself not clear as to what exactly Aristotle meant thereby. Accordingly, he put his own interpretation upon the matter, assuming that tragedy may evoke *either* pity *or* fear, not necessarily both. Poetry must, admittedly, conform to the " rules," but it may be necessary to " tame " these in order to secure a pleasurable end. As for the unities, that of action is essential to a play, and may be secured by various means, such as *liaison* of act and scene. The unity of time, defined by Aristotle as " a single revolution of the sun," Corneille interprets as twenty-four hours or, with latitude, thirty. As for the unity of place, first recognized by Castelvetro in 1570, Corneille adopts this only with modification : " Les jurisconsultes admettent des fictions de droit; et je voudrois, à leur exemple, introduire des fictions de théâtre, pour établir un lieu théâtral "—a conventional spot free from certain dramatic restrictions. On the other hand, Corneille's *invraisemblance* was a poor substitute for *vraisemblance*, however inadequately this latter may have rendered the Aristotelian " impossible—probable."

One other critic of Dryden's period may be mentioned, Saint-Évremond, exiled in England for more than forty years. Saint-Évremond's claim to greatness rests particularly on his contributions to comparative criticism. He praises both Corneille and Racine, but with discrimination : " Corneille se fait admirer par l'expression d'une grandeur d'âme héroïque, par la force des passions, par la sublimité du discours. Racine trouve son mérite en des sentiments plus naturels, en des pensées plus nettes, dans une diction plus pure et plus facile. Le premier enlève l'âme, l'autre gagne l'esprit." He discusses English comedy, finding it apt in the reproduction of ordinary life, and less prone to mere gallantry than either French or Spanish : " Pour ceux qui aiment le ridicule : qui prennent plaisir à bien connoître le faux des esprits : qui sont touchés des vrai caractères, ils trouveront les belles comédies des Anglais selon leur goût, autant et peut-être plus qu'aucunes qu'ils aient jamais vues." Saint-Évremond sought relaxation rather than instruction in books, and found this pre-eminently in Latin. He confessed to a life-long passion for 'Don Quixote, while his favourite French authors were Malherbe, Voiture, Corneille, and Montaigne.

In Dryden the rules of French critics occupy as much space as those of the ancients, English criticism having been moulded under the influence of both. But Dryden had certain temperamental peculiarities which distinguish him from the thorough-going classicists. He, everywhere, reserved for himself the right of independent judgment, and if he followed the rules he followed them " at a distance " (Preface to *Don Sebastian*). He remained an unconvinced adherent of the schools, and it is the romantic element, blended with his classicism, that imparts to his essays their peculiar charm. He refused to surrender English tragi-comedy in favour of French, and gloried in the achievement of Shakespeare. In common with his critical contemporaries, Dryden adopted an objective view of letters, so that the formal criticism of the *Essay of Dramatic Poesy* came opportunely. It presented a .conception of a widely extended republic of letters, in which, though individual taste might go by the board, the great end would be achieved, the amelioration of society at large. Fortunately, Dryden's taste compelled him to admire other than the recognized standards. He preferred Homer to Virgil, Juvenal to Horace, set Chaucer alongside of Ovid, and was convinced that " to err with honest Shakespeare " was no literary crime.

Neander's reply to Lisideius in the *Essay* consequently resolved itself into a duel with Corneille, who, by putting his own interpretation upon the *dicta* of Aristotle, had imparted a colour of its own to French drama. Relying upon the hypothesis that " imitation of nature is the chief thing," Dryden justifies English tragi-comedy on the ground that " contraries set off each other," and defends the underplot in a fine simile, " Our plays, besides the main design, have under-plots or by-concernments of less considerable persons and intrigues, which are carried on with the motion of the main plot : as they say the orb of fixed stars, and those of the planets, though they have motions of their own, are whirled about by the motion of the *primum mobile*, in which they are contained. If contrary motions may be found in nature to agree, it will not be difficult to imagine how the under-plot may naturally be conducted along with it." Again, Dryden has no great admiration for Corneille's declamatory speeches which tire by their length. But if English methods are generally defensible, he allows that tumults on the stage are a mere concession to the audience. As for the unities, these constitute a troublesome affair, and even Corneille admitted that one may be over-punctilious. In any case, the French theory of a *lieu théâtral* is altogether too fantastic.

While Dryden was composing his miscellaneous prefaces and essays, a critic of a different stamp, Thomas Rymer, was engaged on a translation of Rapin and a *Short View of Tragedy*. Though Macaulay described Rymer as " the worst critic that ever lived," he won recognition in his day, and there are elements in his work which have, at least, historical importance. Thus, with reference to Aristotle, Rymer wrote in his *Preface to Rapin* : " The truth is, what Aristotle writes on this subject are not the dictates of his own magisterial will, or dry deductions of his metaphysics. But the poets were his masters, and what was their practice he reduced to principles." This is less dogmatic than his later assertion : (His reasons) " are convincing and clear as any demonstration in mathematics," and, though Rymer was a thorough-going Aristotelian, it is upon principles of what he called " common sense " that he claims to found his criticism. He had, at any rate, one side of the critic's equipment—some knowledge of literary history. If he omits Chaucer, on the ground that his language was not " capable of any heroic character," he recalls the fact that the fourteenth century was the period when Petrarch attempted " the epic strain in his *Africa*." Naturally, he is not over-enthusiastic regarding Spenser, who made " no conscience of probability " and fell upon an " unlucky choice " of stanza, but his genius is admitted and his poem pronounced " perfect fairyland " (the exact force being, of course, dubious). He recognizes Davenant's wit and Cowley's majesty of style, with the qualification that the former's heroes were aliens, and the latter indiscreet in his selection of a sacred theme for epic. He concludes with a number of passages descriptive of " night," culled from Virgil, Tasso, and Chapelain, side by side with an English excerpt from the *Conquest of Mexico*, which appears to him to be as felicitous as any. This first attempt to institute a comparison by actual concrete illustration must be set to Rymer's credit, and, if he be " the worst critic that ever lived," it is assuredly not here but to his *Short View of Tragedy* that one must look.

III

MILTON

IF Shakespeare is the greatest of English romantic poets, Milton is pre-eminent among the classical. He is the high-priest of English classicism, and classicism differentiates itself from romanticism mainly in the sense that Milton differentiates himself from Shakespeare. The classic method, in its widest sense, finds illustration in that passage in the seventh book of *Paradise Lost*, which Addison cites as an example of the sublime :

> On Heavenly ground they stood, and from the shore
> They viewed the vast immeasurable abyss,
> Outrageous as a sea, dark, wasteful, wild,
> Up from the bottom turned by furious winds
> And surging waves, as mountains to assault
> Heaven's heights, and with the centre mix the pole.

The combination of abstract and concrete, the use of figure and comparison, the rejection of suggestion and parable in favour of episode and simile, the preference for the comprehensive and vague rather than the particular and detailed, characteristic of *Paradise Lost*, are characteristic of the classic method, in general. The eighteenth century methods of Pope and his school, inspired though they were by less lofty ideals, were yet a heritage from an earlier period, and owed their being, largely, to Milton.

Milton's precocity was at once apparent in his boyish love of reading, which kept him up " commonly till twelve or one o'clock at night." At the same time, the sights which the city afforded left vivid impressions on his mind, and his later poems abound in metaphors derived from the Thames. His experiments in Greek and Latin versification began early, and are not without signs of that elegance, which the poet was afterwards to import into the " harsh and grating Brittonic idiom." Of his English paraphrases of the *Psalms*, composed according to his own account at the age of fifteen, nothing need be said other than that they are narrative poems in the spirit of Sylvester's *Du Bartas*, and, though they display some skill in diction and versification, are mainly concessions to Puritan standards.

> The ruddy waves he cleft in twain,
> Of the Erythraean main,
> For his mercies aye endure,
> Ever faithful, ever sure,

—these are typical lines.

The ascendancy which the young scholar was to gain over his companions at Cambridge is already apparent in *At a Vacation Exercise*, composed in 1628 as an address to his fellow-students. According to traditional custom, the poet assumes the rôle of " Father," the rest bearing to him the relationship of " sons." The greater portion of the address is in Latin, but, towards the end, Milton turns to English—the " Native language, that by sinews weak (did) move my first endeavouring tongue to speak." His defence of the vernacular is the more important, inasmuch as it marked a departure from the regular theme, to which he feels compelled to return :

> But fie! my wandering Muse, how thou dost stray!
> Expectance calls thee now another way,
> Thou know'st it must be now thy only bent
> To keep in compass of thy predicament,

and he proceeds, scholastically, with the Aristotelian doctrine of the relationship between the eternal substance and its accidents.

In the following year (1629) a happier theme occupied the poet's imagination, and, in an ingenious metre of his own invention, he wrote the hymn, *On the Morning of Christ's Nativity*. Its rich romantic diction is reminiscent of Spenser, to whom, according to Dryden, Milton acknowledged obligations. There is, besides, a tendency to employ words in an etymological sense— " unexpressive " for " inexpressible," " awful " for " timid," " to strike a universal peace " in imitation of the Latin *icere foedus*, together with occasional lapses into artificiality and conceits, and this despite the fact that Milton had already, in the *Vacation Exercise*, finally eschewed

> Those new-fangled toys, and trimmings slight,
> Which takes our late fantastics with delight.

The theme admitted of wide classical and Biblical allusion, and the skill, with which Milton in the twenty-second and succeeding stanzas handles his names, affords an early indication of the mastery he was soon to attain over what has been termed the *science des noms*.

To the Cambridge period belong, likewise, the poem on the *Passion*, the worst example of Milton's employment of conceits, the lines on Shakespeare, afterwards prefixed to the folio edition of 1632, the tender epitaph on the Marchioness of Winchester, and Milton's isolated attempt at humour in the lines, *On the University Carrier*.

In that model of what a literary biography ought not to be, Johnson ruthlessly revived the tradition that, for some insubordination or other, Milton suffered corporal punishment at Cambridge. In view of the political and literary hostility between the poet and his biographer, it seems fair to conclude that Johnson's " I am ashamed to relate " was not altogether unbiassed. Milton's general impression of Cambridge does not seem, at any rate, to have rankled in his mind, since he afterwards publicly acknowledged " that more than ordinary respect, which I found, above many of my equals, at the hands of those courteous and learned men, the Fellows of that college wherein I spent some years." In the sonnet, *On His Being Arrived at the Age of Twenty-three* (1631), Milton had recorded his ambition to so order his career as "it shall be in strictest measure even To that same lot, however mean or high, Toward which Time leads me, and the will of Heaven." This lofty intent, though it did not lead him into the arms of the Church, at least inspired him to dedicate himself to the service of art with all the seriousness of a lofty purpose : "He who would not be frustrated of his hope to write well hereafter in laudable things ought himself to be a true poem . . . not presuming to sing high praises of heroic men or famous cities, unless he have in himself the experience and practice of all that which is praiseworthy."

The formative period in Milton's poetic life was now over, and, during the six years at Horton, he produced work, which he never surpassed in its own manner. There have not been wanting critics to assert that Milton's finest achievement belongs to this period, that in *Lycidas*, for example, he reached his high-water mark. To this there is but one reply—that, without *Paradise Lost* and its successors, the real Milton would be for ever concealed from us. We may, however, rejoice that for a period Milton was able to solace his mind with thoughts redolent of youth and joyfulness; the period soon passed, never to return.

The earliest of the poems written at Horton appear to have been *L'Allegro* and *Il Penseroso*, portraits of the joyful and the contemplative man. In form and diction they are closely akin, both opening with an invocation in stanzaic form, and developing their themes in octosyllables. But, in subject, *L'Allegro* and *Il Penseroso* offer a striking antithesis, such as might have arisen in the poet's mind under the influence of opposing moods. Yet the treatment of the contemplative man seems the more sympathetic, since, as Johnson expressed it : " No mirth can indeed be found in his melancholy, but I am afraid that I always meet some melancholy in his mirth." With admirable technical skill, Milton varies the general flow of his octosyllables in accordance with his theme—the metre of *L'Allegro* advancing with a light tripping movement, that of *Il Penseroso* with heavy steps. The conclusion of *L'Allegro*,

> These delights if thou canst give,
> Mirth, with thee I mean to live,

certainly suggests less confidence than that of the companion poem :

> These pleasures, Melancholy, give,
> And I with thee will choose to live.

The new interest in nature which came into the poet's life at Horton lends colour to both. But Milton was apt to see nature through the spectacles of books, and his epithets lie open to such objections as it pleased Mark Pattison to urge. *Arcades* and *Comus*, Milton's contributions to the masque, were presented, the former before the Dowager Countess of Derby at Harefield, the latter before her son-in-law, the Earl of Bridgewater. *Arcades* is the first of the poems, preserved in the valuable Miltonic manuscripts at Trinity College, Cambridge. How Milton came to write either is unknown, but the fact that his friend, Lawes, was responsible for the music suggests their origin. *Arcades* (1633) is, unfortunately, but a fragment consisting of three songs and a poetical address; it pales alongside *Comus* (1634), the metrical qualities of which set it in the very forefront of Milton's early work. Nothing in English literature is superior in exquisiteness of diction and metre to the songs in *Comus*, or the speech addressed to the rout of monsters :

> The star that bids the shepherd fold
> Now the top of heaven doth hold;
> And the gilded car of day
> His glowing axle doth allay

> In the steep Atlantic stream;
> And the slope sun his upward beam
> Shoots against the dusky pole;
> Pacing toward the other goal
> Of his chamber in the east.
> Meanwhile welcome joy and feast,
> Midnight shout and revelry,
> Tipsy dance and jollity.

Even Johnson was forced to admit that " a work more truly poetical is rarely found; allusions, images and descriptive epithets embellish every period with lavish decoration," though, unfortunately, he afterwards qualified this by asserting that " the songs are harsh in their diction and not very musical in their numbers."

Johnson was nearer the truth in characterizing the dramatic side of the poem as deficient, though he did not always hit upon the weak spots—such as Milton's tendency to employ his characters as mouthpieces of his own opinions. The political doctrines, expounded by the lady in the presence of Comus, seem out of place in a dramatic dialogue, and savour too much of platform oratory :

> If every just man that now pines with want,
> Had but a moderate and becoming share
> Of that which lewdly-pampered Luxury
> Now heaps upon some few with vast excess,
> Nature's full blessings would be well dispersed
> In unsuperfluous even proportion,
> And she no whit encumbered with her store.

Similarly with the speeches, in which the elder brother seeks to prove the self-protective nature of chastity, though it is to these very passages that Milton relegates his central doctrine :

> But evil on itself shall back recoil
> And mix no more with goodness, when at last
> Gathered like scum, and settled to itself,
> It shall be in eternal restless change,
> Self-fed and self-consumed. If this fail,
> The pillared firmament is rottenness,
> And earth's base built on stubble.

The Horton period came to an end with the composition of *Lycidas* (1637), along with which it is convenient to mention a number of poems, composed between 1632-8—*Upon the Circumcision, On Time,* and *At a Solemn Music.* *Lycidas,* a pastoral elegy on the death of Edward King, drowned off the Welsh coast in August, 1637, is the first of a line, represented by *Adonais, Thyrsis,* and *In Memoriam,* and shares with *Comus* the honour of being the highest achievement of the Horton period. Johnson's astounding strictures upon this delicate piece of work recoil upon his own head, and serve to indicate the limits of eighteenth century poetic ideals. He finds " the diction harsh, the rhymes uncertain, and the numbers unpleasing. . . . The form is that of a pastoral—easy, vulgar, and therefore disgusting " (i.e., distasteful). If it be conceded that ecclesiastical controversy plays too large a part in the poem, and that the classical allusions are remote from the main theme, this amounts to little beside such a passage as the following, in which the poet modestly excuses himself for having undertaken a task, to which he felt his powers unequal :

> Yet once more, O ye laurels, and once more,
> Ye myrtles brown, with ivy never sere,
> I come to pluck your berries harsh and crude,
> And with forced fingers rude
> Shatter your leaves before the mellowing year.
> Bitter constraint and sad occasion dear
> Compels me to disturb your season due;
> For Lycidas is dead, dead ere his prime,
> Young Lycidas, and hath not left his peer.

" To scorn delights and live laborious days " had become a regulative principle with Milton, and the poem may be regarded as a link between his early joyous poetry and that serious life-task, for which everything now served as a preparation. The question

> Were it not better done, as others use
> To sport with Amaryllis in the shade,
> Or with the tangles of Neaera's hair?

had by this time been solved for the poet.

II. *PARADISE LOST* AND *SAMSON AGONISTES*

In considering Milton's poetical achievement it is unnecessary to enter in any detail into an account of the political struggles, in which he played so prominent a part. But the experiences of the Civil Wars were of no slight significance in the moulding of the poet's mind. They drew from him the most intense of the sonnets—that to the Lord General Cromwell, burning with a passion for religious liberty,

> Help us to save free conscience from the paw
> Of hireling wolves, whose gospel is their maw,

the other, *On the Late Massacre in Piedmont* (1655), a cry of despair on behalf of an oppressed people :

> Forget not, in thy book record their groans,
> Who were thy sheep, and in their ancient fold
> Slain by the bloody Piedmontese that rolled
> Mother with infant down the rocks.

They drew from him, besides, the masterly pamphlets, hot with scorn and passion, wherein he sought to establish the foundations of civil and religious liberty. History supplies us with few, if any, examples of poets, who have comported themselves with success in the political arena, and Milton's escapades are still regarded askance. It is sufficient to assert that, apart from the experiences reflected in the prose works, the later epics would have lacked their salient characteristics. The germ of *Paradise Lost* grew up in the soil of political controversy, and actually found prose settings in the *Reason of Church Government* and in *Areopagitica.* " It was from out the rind of one apple tasted," so runs a passage in the latter, " that the knowledge of good and evil, as two twins cleaving together, leaped forth into the world." The date of publication, 1667, marks the mere crowning point of a long preparation of thirty years, during which Milton had meditated his theme. The diffidence, with which he approached *Lycidas,* suggests that, as far back as 1637, he considered himself unworthy of the laudable theme which had become his ambition. Nor was the theme itself discovered without much heart-burning. The famous Trinity College manuscript records a list of nearly a hundred subjects, which suggested themselves at different times to Milton's mind : some scriptural—the Deluge, Samson in Ramath Lechi, a pastoral out of Ruth, the death of John the Baptist; some from Old English history—" Cynewulf, king of the West Saxons, slain by Cyneheard in the house of one of his concubines," etc. others from Scottish history—" Macbeth, beginning with the arrival of Malcolm at Mackduffe (the matter of Duncan may be express't by the appearing of his ghost)," etc. But, side by side with these, there are four distinct drafts for a poem on *Paradise Lost*—one arranged dramatically in five acts. It is interesting to conjecture what Milton would have made of the subject of Arthur, had he adopted the theme which first suggested itself. But, apart from speculation, evidence of enthusiasm for the Celtic legend is clearly traceable in the decorative embroidery of *Paradise Lost* itself :

> what resounds
> In fable or romance of Uther's son
> Begirt with British and Armoric knights.

There are, at least, two distinct ways of approaching the study of *Paradise Lost*. We may bring to it our receipt for an epic poem, derived from the study of Aristotle and earlier epic, and so test it by its conformity with the " rules." Or we may approach it receptively, so as to permit its spirit to permeate our minds. Our impressions will then need to be compared with those aroused by wider reading in the same direction. Whichever test be applied, *Paradise Lost* emerges triumphantly, though with greater qualification in the former case. The first method—that of testing according to preconceived notions of what an epic ought to be—is illustrated in the comments of Addison and Johnson.

They examine, in turn, the subject, the sentiments, the diction, the machinery, and, despite various strictures, are in accord with the general conclusions of later criticism. " Everything that is great in the whole circle of being," says Addison, " whether within the verge of nature or out of it, have a proper part assigned to it in this admirable poem," and Johnson concludes: " Such is the power of his poetry, that his call is obeyed without resistance, the reader feels himself in captivity to a higher and a nobler mind, and criticism sinks in admiration."

Paradise Lost ranks side by side with the *Iliad,* the *Æneid,* and the *Divine Comedy* among world-epics. Compared with the *Iliad,* or with primitive Germanic poetry, its artistic side emerges into greater prominence —it belongs to the class of artificial rather than popular epic, in which spontaneous expression is given to the life of a people. Yet, as it is the function of a poet to impart to " the age and body of the time his form and pressure," *Paradise Lost* is itself a reflection of the various ideals—Hebraic and Hellenic—that swayed the poet's period. From a theological standpoint, it is less impartial than the *Divine Comedy,* which recognized but two authorities in the temporal and spiritual realms —the Emperor and the Pope. The difference is a difference of epoch ; on the one hand, a period of homogeneous religious belief, on the other, of violent sectarian opposition, of which Milton's ardent Puritanism was but a phase. Yet the local and temporary character of its theology constitutes no blemish in *Paradise Lost.* The combination of local and universal was precisely what was needed to make the poem both an accurate representation of contemporary society and a work for all time. Still, the fact that Milton was, more or less, an advocate for a particular theological system imposed limitations, and it is impossible to agree with Addison that *Paradise Lost* surpasses the *Æneid* and the *Iliad,* merely because it determines not " the fate of single

persons or nations, but of a whole species." Further,
the subject offered difficulties from an artistic point of
view. The characters are both men and angels, and, in
the attempt to give concrete representation to the latter,
Milton proved inconsistent. To serve the ends of art,
the angel of the Lord must needs assume humanity, but
Milton's spiritual philosophy admits a dualism, whereby
angels

> in what shape they choose,
> Dilated or condensed, bright or obscure,
> Can execute their airy purposes
> And works of love or enmity fulfil.

In Johnson's words, the angels are " sometimes pure
spirit, and sometimes animated body." The realm of
universal space which Milton chose for his theatre
involved similar difficulties. Chaos is strictly describable
in merely negative terms, though here the strength of
Milton's method found magnificent illustration :

> I saw when at his word the formless mass,
> This world's material mould, came to a heap:
> Confusion heard his voice, and wild uproar
> Stood ruled, stood vast infinitude confused;
> Till at his second bidding Darkness fled,
> Light shone, and order from disorder sprung.

But the method of concrete representation must needs
be applied at some point, and Milton proceeded to map
out the boundaries of Heaven, Earth, and Hell with the
skill of a geometer. His cosmical conceptions are
dominated, on the whole, by the old astronomy and the
old physics. The earth is at the centre of the spheres,
on which the planets turn, a " pendent world, in bigness
as a star of smallest magnitude, close by the moon." Its
constitution is made up of the four elements, Cold,
Hot, Dry and Moist, compounded from Earth, Air, Fire
and Water. As for his theology, it transcends the limits
of the Bible, and is traceable to the *Book of Enoch*, the
Apocalypse of Moses, the *Zohar*, and other obscure

sources. Even his *De Doctrina Christiana* is saturated by the Arianism, reflected in the epic.

It is a tribute to the greatness of *Paradise Lost* that, even in the eyes of classical critics, its merits bulked larger than its defects. The revived interest in Milton during the eighteenth century was mainly due to Addison, who contributed to the *Spectator,* on alternate Saturdays from January to May, 1712, a series of *causeries* on *Paradise Lost.* These are of interest—less, perhaps, from the . critical standpoint than from that of enthusiastic appreciation. Reason has been found to quarrel with Addison's view that Milton's theme is great, precisely because it determines the fate of " a whole species." On the other hand, if Adam be regarded as the perfect man, Aristotelian canons demand that we look elsewhere for a hero, and, with Shelley and Dryden, raise Satan to that high eminence. Whatever interest the happy pair in Eden may have for posterity will depend upon the vestiges of humanity they display, since, with some perversion of Addison's meaning, " we are embarked with them on the same bottom, and must be partakers of their happiness or misery." Nor is our difference with Addison ended, when he proceeds to catalogue the defects of the poem—its unhappy event, its digressions, the improbable characters of Sin and Death. For it is precisely the taint of sorrow at the close that unites Adam and Eve with the rest of humanity, and Milton has exquisitely realized the pathos of the situation :

> They, hand in hand, with wandering steps and slow,
> Through Eden took their solitary way.

Nor may we lightly surrender the twin figures of Sin and Death, conceived by De Quincey as " prompted by secret sympathy, and snuffing the distant scent of mortal change on earth, chasing the steps of their great progenitor and sultan." As for the digressions, they constitute the poem's chief ornament. Addison is justified, however, in his condemnation of the trifling puns and jingles,

And brought into the world a world of woe.

At one slight bound high overleaped all bound,

which served Milton as a substitute for humour. But, when it is a question of appreciation, Addison is no niggard, and there are few collections of " beauties " to vie with the Milton papers in the *Spectator*. It is upon its artistic qualities that the permanent greatness of *Paradise Lost* depends—qualities such as revealed themselves earlier in *Comus* and *Lycidas*. The epic device of the simile served in Milton's hands the purpose of decorative ornament. Debarred by the nature of his theme from a world of ideas, he had recourse to a device, whereby he enhanced his poem with all the pomp of learning and imagination. The similes *de longue haleine* are ever in keeping with the emotional tone, and constitute perhaps the most striking feature of *Paradise Lost*. Thus, the descriptions of Satan's oratory, the building of Pandemonium, and the legions of evil spirits are reinforced and enhanced with the most apposite of classical, scientific, and natural illustrations. Consummate mastery over technical effects of rhythm is as characteristic of *Paradise Lost* as of the Horton poems, and the paragraphs break into a lyric harmony, unsurpassed elsewhere. Eve's description of her dream, followed by the Morning Hymn in Book V, and her speech in Book IV, " Sweet is the breath of morn, her rising sweet," produce an entirely lyrical effect. The autobiographical passages have the added touch of experience—the mellowness that comes with age:

> Thus with the year
> Seasons return; but not to me returns
> Day, or the sweet approach of even or morn,
> Or sight of vernal bloom, or summer's rose,
> Or flocks or herds, or human face divine:
> But cloud instead, and everduring dark
> Surrounds me, from the cheerful ways of men
> Cut off, and from the book of knowledge fair.
> (Book III.)

It is well known that the germ of *Paradise Regained*

is traceable to a remark of Thomas Ellwood's, when Milton was living at Chalfont St. Giles in 1665: " Thou hast said much here of *Paradise Lost,* but what hast thou to say of *Paradise Found?* " In reality, *Paradise Lost* needed no sequel. The significant prophecy of Book X—" Her seed shall bruise thy head, thou bruise his heel "—had been an integral part of the poem. But a concession must needs be made to the weaker brethren, and Milton adopted Ellwood's suggestion, elaborating it into *Paradise Regained* (published 1671, though finished some five years earlier). In his new epic Milton limited himself to an episode in the career of the Saviour—the temptation in the wilderness. His choice was dictated by artistic considerations. It enabled him to bring Christ and the old enemy of Adam into vivid juxtaposition—the situation was at once typical and representative. Milton's treatment of the scene in the wilderness owed something to Giles Fletcher's religious poem, *Christ's Triumph on Earth,* which, opening with a description of Christ's sojourn in the desert, proceeded, rapidly, to the first temptation. There are further affinities with *Paradise Regained* in the later portions of the poem, but Fletcher's allegorical method differentiates him *toto caelo* from Milton.

The style of *Paradise Regained* is less imaginative than that of the companion epic, and its rigorous asceticism eschews embroidery. In three instances only —the banquet scene, the descriptions of Rome and Athens, and the storm in Book IV—does Milton permit himself latitude. Lamb found the banquet scene " too civic and culinary, and the accompaniments altogether a profanation of that deep, abstracted and holy scene "—sound criticism, provided the extreme beauty of the passage be admitted, and the skill, with which Milton has emphasized, by contrast, the utter dreariness of the desert. The attack on Greek literature and philosophy, again, comes strangely from one who was himself steeped in classical learning. Milton wilfully misrepresents the teachings of pagan philosophy, casting a slur upon ancient music and poetry in his endeavour to exalt the songs of Sion. Yet, as Satan convincingly put it :

> All knowledge is not couch'd in Moses' law,
> The pentateuch, or what the Prophets wrote;
> The Gentiles also know and write and teach
> To admiration, led by Nature's light.

Paradise Regained has never won the affection of readers to the same extent as *Paradise Lost*, yet the poet himself was unable to bear with patience any disparagement of his later epic.

The poem, with which Milton closed his career, represents his greatest concession to antiquity. The romantic admixture, with which in *Paradise Lost* he had tempered the austerity of his classicism, is wholly lacking in *Samson Agonistes*, which is Greek in form and diction. Milton's source—the simple narrative of *Judges* —was enlarged with details from Josephus. That he owed anything to earlier literary settings, Boccaccio's *De casibus illustrium virorum*, Chaucer's *Monk's Tale*, or Lydgate's *Falls of Princes*, cannot be shown. In meditating the theme of *Paradise Lost*, Milton had hesitated between the claims of epic and drama, and made his choice only after long experiment. Now, at the close of his career, he definitely adopted the dramatic form, embodying in it the deepest of his personal experiences. Having detected a dramatic outline in the *Song of Solomon*, " a Divine pastoral drama . . . consisting of two persons and a double chorus," he had no scruples in handling a religious theme dramatically. The tragedy of *Samson Agonistes* was, however, no concession to the Caroline stage—it was rather a protest, since it was the austere style and form of Greek, rather than of English tragedy, that Milton adopted. The three unities—of time, place, and action—are carefully observed, in deference to what was conceived to be the Aristotelian position. The time does not exceed twenty-four hours, the scene is laid outside the prison at Gaza, the action tends inevitably towards the catastrophe. The chorus, in accordance with the practice of Sophocles, takes a share in the action. Rhyme is largely eschewed as " the invention of a barbarous age to set off wretched matter and lame metre." In opposition to Johnson and Macaulay, it may be maintained that *Samson Agonistes* is, from the purely literary standpoint, a magnificent achievement. The dialogues alone contain passages of exquisite beauty, e.g., Samson's premonition of death :

> Nature within me seems
> In all her functions weary of herself;
> My race of glory run, and race of shame,
> And I shall shortly be with them that rest,

or old Manoa's cry of despair :

> What windy joy this day had I conceived,
> Hopeful of his delivery, which now proves
> Abortive as the first-born bloom of spring,
> Nipt with the lagging rear of winter's frost.

But the quintessence of the poetry has been relegated to the choruses, in which Macaulay perceived nothing but " wild and barbarous melody." These are, with difficulty, reduced to type; they are irregular in both feet and length of line, employing rhyme on occasion, with no apparent purpose. The freedom, at which Milton aimed, was, no doubt, suggested by the Greek choruses, where the conduct of the paragraph was dictated by emotional considerations. The freedom is, therefore, only apparent—paragraph, line, and foot being, one and all, adapted for emotional expression. Tried by this test, the choruses of *Samson Agonistes* prove to be " magnificently harmonious," " consummate specimens of English verse."

> Go, and the Holy One
> Of Israel be thy guide
> To what may serve his glory best, and spread his name
> Great among the Heathen round;
> Send thee the Angel of thy birth, to stand

Fast by thy side, who from thy father's field
Rode up in flames after his message told
Of thy conception, and be now a shield
Of fire; that Spirit that first rushed on thee
In the camp of Dan,
Be efficacious in thee now at need!

Samson Agonistes is an autobiographical poem, with Milton as its centre.   At the same time, it is a national poem, representative of England under Charles II.   But its dominant quality is Greek, and, from this standpoint, it reveals, in Goethe's words, "more of the antique spirit than any production of any other modern poet."

IV

BROWNE'S *RELIGIO MEDICI*

SIR THOMAS BROWNE ranks, as a prose writer, with the greatest of the makers of Caroline literature. At his best, the peer of Milton and Taylor, he is distinguished from them by various idiosyncrasies, while his style, a product of the pre-Augustan period, has nothing in common with the clear precision of Dryden. The hyper-Latinism, with which Coleridge charged Browne, was justified by the author himself, on the ground that " the quality of the subject will sometimes carry us into expressions beyond mere English apprehensions." It may certainly be affirmed that the *Religio Medici* affords one of the finest examples of that wedding of sound to sense, which is among the main requisites of style. Browne's quaintness, his large erudition, his curious speculations in the bypaths of knowledge demanded a vocabulary in keeping. Hence, the exotic terms, the Grecisms, Latinisms, and borrowings from contemporary Romance languages. Yet the *Religio Medici* is never servilely classical, despite monstrosities, like ephemerides, antiperistasis, vespillo, etc. Browne holds himself well in hand, and not until his last years do tricks of style show tendencies to master him. He was a careful reviser, his manuscripts affording evidence of elaboration and refining, and this made him a model for kindred intellects of the type of Lamb and De Quincey. Indeed, apart from the musical and ornate medium of the *Religio Medici*, with its recondite and quaint self-expression, English literature might have missed some of the choicest passages in Elia's writings.

The personal characteristics of the author reveal themselves in the somewhat desultory manner of the *Religio Medici*, in its love of paradox and religious quietism. Browne's humour is not too obvious, but he abounds in wit. His quaintness endears him to every lover of the curious. That the term " Brownism " should have been employed in the eighteenth century with contemptuous force is merely a proof that the worst exaggerations of his Latinized diction were recalled to the prejudice of the finer elements in his style. Of this Latinism the *Religio Medici* affords abundant illuśtration ; instance the involved definition of Providence : " There is another way, full of meanders and labyrinths, whereof the devil and spirits have no exact ephemerides : and that is a more particular and obscure method of his providence ; directing the operations of individual and single essences ; this we call fortune ; that serpentine and crooked line whereby he draws those actions his wisdom intends in a more unknown and secret way ; this cryptic and involved method of his providence have I ever admired ; nor can I relate the history of my life, the occurrences of my days, the escapes, or dangers, and hints of chance, without a *bezo las manos* to Fortune, or a bare gramercy to my good stars." But this Latinism has a fascination of its own. With the enthusiasm of a kindred spirit, Browne lightens his pages with excerpts from his favourite authors, scarcely falling short of their exaltation in his English renderings : " I cannot but marvel from what sibyl or oracle they stole the prophecy of the world's destruction by fire, or whence Lucan learned to say :

> Communis mundo superest rogus, ossibus astra
> Misturus—

> There yet remains to th' world one common fire,
> Wherein our bones with stars shall make one pyre.

Nor does he abate a jot of his enthusiasm for the isolated Latin phrase, though quick to supply an interpretation : thus, " *Natura nihil agit frustra*, is the only indisputable axiom in philosophy. There are no grotesques in nature; not anything framed to fill up empty cantons and unnecessary spaces," or again : " In my solitary and retired imagination (neque enim cum porticus aut me lectulus accepit desum mihi) I remember I am not alone; and therefore forget not to contemplate him and his attributes, who is ever with me, especially those two mighty ones, his wisdom and eternity." With single words his methods vary, and, side by side, with the couplings—" cenotaph or sepulchre," " reflex or shadow," " fougade or powder-pot," " panoplia or complete armour," " catholicon or universal remedy," there are the more elaborate bracketings—" descriptions, periphrasis, or adumbration "; " colusses and majestick pieces of her hand "; " anthropophagi and cannibals, devourers not only of men, but of ourselves "; " anatomies, skeletons, or cadaverous relicks "; and it is clear that Browne's synonyms are designed to enlarge and intensify his impressions. That he was skilled in the subtle ·distinctions of words is evident from the following : " to be particular, I am of that reformed new-cast religion, wherein I dislike nothing but the name, of the same belief our Saviour taught, the apostles disseminated, the fathers authorized, and the martyrs confirmed." Characteristic of his style is alliteration, whether simple or crossed, antithesis, and parallelism—" I condemn not all things in the council of Trent, nor approve all in the synod of Dort. In brief, where the Scripture is silent, the church is my text; where that speaks, 'tis but my comment; where there is a joint silence of both, I borrow not the rules of my religion from Rome or Geneva, but from the dictates of my own reason." With all this, there is a subtle employment of familiar language, evidently designed to secure relief, e.g., " those vulgar heads that look asquint on the face of truth "; " sturdy doubts and boisterous objections "; " a fit of the stone or colick "; " nauseous to queasy stomachs," etc., together with a homely set of metaphors derived from chess, hawking, etc.

That Browne could handle a purely Saxon vocabulary with simple directness is evident, however, from such passages as the following : " Thus we are men, and we know not how; there is something in us, that can be without us, and will be after us, though it is strange that it hath no history what it was before us, nor cannot tell how it entered in us," or, from the *Christian Morals* : " The world which took but six days to make is like to take six thousand to make out."

The *Religio Medici* was published surreptitiously in 1642, the first authorized edition in 1643. Though the author spoke regretfully of the additions, omissions, and transpositions in the pirated edition, research has proved these to be few and unimportant. Sir Kenelm Digby, for one, was so captivated that he made the book his bedfellow, and could not close his eyes till he had enriched himself with " all the treasures that are lapped up in the folds of those few sheets." Nor was the world, at large, less moved. Two Latin editions were printed at Leyden and Paris in 1644, and it was subsequently translated into French, German, and Dutch.

The *Religio Medici* is a defence of a scientific man's attitude towards religion. Of the fundamental Christian verities Browne entertained no doubt; he permitted himself speculation merely on the outskirts of truth. Relying to a great extent upon authority—the authority of the Church no less than that of Scripture—he was, first and foremost, a loyal adherent of the establishment. Thus, in divinity he loved " to keep the road ; and though not in an implicit, yet an humble faith, follow the great wheel of the Church." At the same time, recognizing that the Church of God cannot be wrapped up " in Strabo's cloak and reclaimed unto Europe," he was preserved from such prejudices as often cause men to " excommunicate from heaven one another."

Browne becomes intimate, when he propounds his personal reasons for faith. Here the note is mystical and superrational, for to him a mystery proves a veritable source of joy, and the incredible credible just in so far as it lies beyond the reach of intellect. He takes his stand upon his personality, concluding that : " There is surely a piece of divinity in us; something that was before the elements, and owes no homage unto the sun."

But it is on what he calls " points indifferent " that Browne frees himself from authority, and lays himself open to the charge of heresy. In his *Medicus Medicatus* (1645) Alexander Ross ventured to impugn his orthodoxy, and even Coleridge was of opinion that " Sir T. Browne was Spinozist without knowing it." It is perhaps true that his orthodoxy arises out of his practice of keeping religion and science in separate compartments, though the *Religio Medici*, at least, shows no signs of wavering. To borrow a phrase applied to Spinoza, Browne was fundamentally " a God-intoxicated man."

The speculations of the author of the *Religio Medici* were characterized by a mixture of boldness and timidity : Browne was a bundle of irreconcilable contradictions. He begins by defending the speculative position, whence he proceeds to various problems in the solution of which he shows himself either boldly speculative or childishly credulous. That manna " is now plentifully gathered in Calabria " he is aware, but strangles his doubts from fear lest the devil should be striving " to undermine the edifice " of his faith. That there are stories in Scripture " that do excel the fables of poets, and, to a captious reader, sound like Garagantua or Bevis," he admits, yet prides himself still on the rigour of his orthodoxy. On other issues, Browne was broader and in advance of his age. He imagines that an allegorical interpretation of the early chapters of *Genesis* may be necessary, and admits he once fell under the sway of Origen. He permits his imagination to hover around the solemnities of the Last Judgment, rejecting the literal interpretation, on the ground that " unspeakable mysteries in the Scriptures are often delivered in a vulgar and illustrative way, and, being delivered unto man, are delivered not as they truly are, but as they may be understood." His scientific knowledge suggested parallels in the natural world for the mystery of the Resurrection, though he admitted the impossibility in such cases of adducing " any solid or demonstrative reasons." In his views of the future life Browne was distinctly modern, though anticipated in this particular by Omar : " Behold myself am heaven and hell." He speculates on the nature of angels as " light invisible," following this with a pronouncement on man as " that great and true amphibium, whose nature is disposed to live, not only like other creatures in divers elements, but in divided and distinguished worlds." Towards miracles his attitude was conservative; they are to be regarded as tests of faith, and, in raising doubts as to their validity, " we do too narrowly define the power of God, restraining it to our capacities." In the transmutation of the " visible elements into the body and blood of our Saviour " we see a miracle daily repeated. Browne's conservatism prepares us, in some degree, for the discovery that he clung to many of the superstitions of his day. He was credulous regarding ghosts, witchcraft, and chiromancy. Yet to him ghosts were " not the wandering souls of men but the unquiet walks of devils, prompting and suggesting us unto mischief, blood and villainy "; for " the souls of the faithful, when they leave earth, cease to trouble the living." On the other hand, his attitude towards witchcraft contrasts strangely with his general humanity. Sir Kenelm Digby had challenged Browne's assertion regarding the existence of witches. In 1664, however, Browne gave practical proof of his creed by assisting in the condemnation of two unfortunates, accused of having used sorcery for the injury of young children. This remains an unhappy blot on his career.

The *Religio Medici*, by its autobiographical character, has proved invaluable as a revelation of its author's personality. Browne belongs to that class of author, the charm of whose writings resides in their intimacy. He is as interested in his own personality as R. L. Stevenson, but conducts the analysis in a manner that is never offensive. His genial egotism constitutes a tribute to the perpetual miracle of existence. It is in man, the microcosm, that the solution of the riddle of the universe is to be found, hence the justification for his genial introspection. Beginning by confessing that he is naturally bashful, he goes on to declare that he is distinguished from his fellows by complete indifference to fear. The violent changes wrought by decay alone disturb him, though, admittedly, he has no reason to be ashamed of the anatomy of his parts, nor can accuse nature of " having played the bungler " with him. Of his personal merits he speaks humbly enough, confessing it to be his sole desire to " be but the last man and bring up the rear in heaven." In the early pages of the *Religio Medici*, his sympathies had led him to regard indulgently all such as stood without the pale of Christianity, and, later, he denies he has any personal antipathies, whatsoever. Lamb's confessed aversion for certain types contrasts curiously with Browne's assertion that " such national repugnances do not touch me, nor do I behold with prejudice the French, Italian, Spaniard or Dutch," and there is, certainly, more of average humanity in his blunt outburst. Yet Browne admits hatred of " that numerous piece of monstrosity," the multitude—" a monstrosity more prodigious than Hydra "—his affection centring rather in the individual, wheresoever he find him. His sympathy is alienated, neither by ignorance nor by intellectual differences. His prayers embrace the whole of his circle; and the mere appearance of death arouses his solicitude. He is touched by the piety and devotion of others; hence his respect for the formalities of the Holy Catholic Church, even though his reason be untouched. Browne can scarcely be accused of exaggeration in those glimpses he has given of his acquired knowledge. That he was familiar with no less than six languages need scarcely be doubted. He probably had some acquaintance with Hebrew and Arabic, in addition to the classics; while his friendship with the Icelander, Theodor Jónsson, may have resulted in some familiarity with the then little-known tongue of Iceland. References to astrology, zoology, and botany abound in his works, and amply justify his statement that he knew " the names and somewhat more of all the constellations in my horizon," and " most of the plants of my country."

Browne's immense erudition is attested by contemporaries. Evelyn gives us a pleasing glimpse of his surroundings at Norwich. His house was a " paradise and cabinet of rarities." Among other curiosities, he had a " collection of the eggs of all the fowl and birds he could procure, that country (especially the promontory of Norfolk) being frequented, as he said, by several kinds which seldom or never go farther into the land, as cranes, storks, eagles, and variety of water-fowl." The pages of *Hydriotaphia* and the *Garden of Cyrus* supply ample evidence of curious learning, and there are the posthumous essays, with their discussions on primitive languages, the site of Troy, and other recondite matters.

In his home circle, Browne appears to have been a kind and tender father, " though," as he himself admits, in " no way facetious, nor disposed for the mirth and galliardise of company." By nature a dreamer, he was moved, above all things, by the contemplation of life, *sub specie æternitatis*. Paradox was his favourite weapon. He gazes on the unfamiliar aspect of things, indulging his imagination with curiosities, and would fain have us believe that "in nature there are no grotesques, nor anything framed to fill up unnecessary spaces."

The views to which Browne gives expression would seem to have necessarily involved a retired atmosphere, and, despite the fact that he displayed considerable activity as a medical practitioner, the dates of his various writings are significant. It was, as J. A. Symonds pointed out, in 1643 (the year of Chalgrove Field) that he published the *Religio Medici*; the *Vulgar Errors* belongs to 1646 (the year of Charles's retreat to the North), while the appearance of *Hydriotaphia* coincided with the death of Cromwell (1658). A certain aloofness from public affairs is, doubtless, indicated by these dates.

V

DRYDEN

I. POEMS AND SATIRES

BETWEEN Milton and Pope there is no figure of the eminence of John Dryden, " the puissant and glorious founder of our excellent and indispensable eighteenth century," and the chief in our second order of poets. Curiosity, insatiably interested in extra-literary matters, has sought to discover whether Dryden came into actual contact with either Milton or Pope. The matter is no longer conjectural. Dryden met Milton, whom he reports as having said : " Spenser is my original "—a piece of information which posterity declines to accept. On the other hand, Spence is the authority for Pope's statement : " I saw Mr. Dryden when I was about twelve years of age : this bust is like him. I remember his face well; for I looked upon him, even then, with the greatest veneration, and observed him very particularly."

The extraordinary inequality of Dryden's verse has impressed every critic, and is explicable merely as a matter of temperament. The inequality within the limits of a single poem is, indeed, more astounding than the contrast afforded by his early and his later work, particular explanations for which might be adduced. Unlike Pope, nurtured in an atmosphere of classical refinement, Dryden was at an early age subjected to influences the very negation of " correct." When, as a pupil at Westminster, he first essayed the art of verse, the influence of Donne was predominant.

The *Elegy on the Death of Lord Hastings* (1649) is, accordingly, disfigured by the grossest conceits, and might almost be considered a parody of the metaphysical manner. Having expatiated on the virtue and learning of this young lord of nineteen,

> His bódy wás an órb, his súblime sóul
> Did move on virtue's and on learning's pole,

Dryden proceeds to denounce the disease, to which he fell a victim :

> Was there no milder way but the small-pox,
> The very filthiness of Pandora's box?
> So many spots, like naeves our Venus soil?
> One jewel set off with so many a foil?
> Blisters with pride swelled, which through his flesh did sprout,
> Like rosebuds, stuck in the lily-skin about.
> Each little pimple had a tear in it
> To wail the fault its rising did commit.

Here, there is no promise of the dawn, unless, indeed, in isolated lines suggestive of the strength of the later Dryden, such as :

> Were fíxed and cónglobate ín his sóul and thénce.

This might have made a good line, while the following actually is such :

> An universal metempsychosis.

Yet three or four good lines scarcely constitute a poem.

These " tears " represent all that is known of Dryden's school experiments, nor does he appear to have written much at Cambridge. The commendatory lines prefixed to Hoddesdon's *Epigrams* in 1650 are slight in bulk, and, though somewhat more accomplished than their predecessors, admit the inevitable conceit in its worst form. No doubt Dryden was drawn to the town soon after his graduation at Cambridge (1654). His income raised him above necessity, and there were circumstances which made his position particularly favourable. The Cromwell party had just risen to power, and Dryden was not likely to escape recognition, while it was remembered how his grandfather, Sir Erasmus Dryden, had resisted Charles's "loans," and his father had aided in ejecting refractory ministers. His cousin, Sir Gilbert Pickering, was a *persona grata* with Cromwell, and the young poet seems to have acted as his secretary. The death of Cromwell in 1658 gave an opportunity to the poets, and, though none equalled the *Ode* written by Marvell in 1650, the contributions of Waller and Dryden were noteworthy. The most interesting fact about Dryden's *Heroic Stanzas* is the adoption of the quatrain as verse-form, whereby the metre of *Annus Mirabilis* was anticipated. For his model, Dryden had Davenant's *Gondibert*, the popular poem of the hour, but his choice was dictated less by popular taste than by a conviction that the quatrain would both allow him freedom, and, at the same time, curb propensities to diffuseness. It combined the freedom of the larger stanza with the restriction of the couplet, which a later poet described as tying "its galling chain" round his "heart's leg." The *Heroic Stanzas* are not entirely free from Dryden's mannerisms, but their anticipations of his later method deserve recognition. They formed a useful exercising-ground for the poet's immaturity :

> He made us freemen of the Continent
> Whom Nature did like captives treat before,
> To nobler preys the English lion sent,
> And taught him first in Belgian walks to roar.

The adulatory stanzas, in which, two years later, Dryden welcomed the new monarch, have often been cited to his detriment, and it is impossible to exonerate him, even though admitting with Johnson that "if he changed, he changed with the nation." Strangely enough, in view of the experiment in the *Heroic Stanzas* and his return to this form in *Annus Mirabilis*, *Astræa Redux*, together with the companion poems, *To His Sacred Majesty* (1661), and *To my Lord Chancellor* (1662), represent a reversion to the couplet. Though

Johnson remarked upon the strained hyperboles, the improper use of mythology, and the occasional irreverence of these poems, he scarcely did justice to their magnificent achievement in the heroic line. Not in isolated examples, but throughout whole paragraphs there is a display of strength such as Dryden never gave evidence of before. Under the spell of his metre, resentment at the poet's change of front is forgotten, and we read with pleasure how

> When our great Monarch into exile went,
> Wit and religion suffered banishment,

or again :

> How great were then our Charles' woes who thus
> Was forced to suffer for himself and us.

If Dryden's rhymes sometimes strike one as faulty, many of them—*wear, fear; prove, love; joined, find*—can be justified on historical grounds. If his matter be mere adulation, the important point is that the poet is here discoverable at work on his grand style.

The first period of Dryden's poetical activity ended with the appearance of *Annus Mirabilis* in 1667. Meanwhile, he had married Sir Robert Howard's sister, and, settling down to his profession, had begun to write plays. He was already a prominent figure in literary circles, and is described by Pepys as participating in the flow of " witty and pleasant discourse " at Will's coffeehouse. In *Annus Mirabilis* there is a reversion to the heroic quatrain, employed in the poem on Cromwell, but the subject offered greater opportunities for the poet's skill. The experience acquired in *Astræa Redux* and its group makes itself felt, and, though no advance is apparent, there is evidence of a new power of descriptive narration. The accounts of the affair at Bergen, of the four days' battle, the repair of the fleet, and the great fire of London are justly famous.

In accordance with what he calls the " general rule in poetry that all appropriated terms of art should be sunk in general expressions," Johnson denounced the technical terms which serve to vivify the dockyard scenes. Regarding which anticipations of the art of Falconer and Kipling, he remarks : " I suppose here is not one term which every reader does not wish away." It is more important to note Dryden's personal defence in the Preface, even though he thought fit to retreat from that position in the dedication to the *Æneid* : " We hear indeed among our poets, of the thundering of guns, the smoke, the disorder and the slaughter, but all these are common notions. And certainly, as those who, in a logical dispute, keep in general terms, would hide a fallacy; so those, who do it in any poetical description, would veil their ignorance." Though the strength of *Annus Mirabilis* consists in the narrative passages, it contains single lines and couplets of remarkable power :

> And weary waves, withdrawing from the fight,
> Lie lulled and panting on the silent shore.
>
> And his loud guns speak thick like angry men.
>
> Each household Genius shows again his face,
> And from the hearths the little Lares creep.

Its faults are lack of unity, an inevitable consequence of the employment of the heroic quatrain, each specimen of which is self-contained and inadequately fused with its neighbours; further, the false taste which disfigures so much contemporary verse.

Between 1668 and 1681, Dryden was mainly occupied with play-writing and left nothing of importance in the domain of pure poetry. His reputation as a man-of-letters had developed rapidly, but, as yet, he had not come into his own. The achievements, whereby he is entitled to rank with Pope among the neo-classic poets, belong to the closing period of his life. In *Absalom and Achitophel*, in the *Medal* and *MacFlecknoe*, in *Religio Laici* and the *Hind and the Panther*, he triumphantly asserted his claim to pre-eminence in the departments of satire and didactic verse. In the first place, these reflect either Dryden's views on current events, his relations with contemporaries, or his personal convictions. *Absalom and Achitophel* (1681), a purely political satire, was based on the old-time story of David and Absalom. The allusions must have been readily apparent to Dryden's contemporaries, who were not slow to identify the Jews with the English, Sion with the English capital, Israel's monarch with Charles II, Saul with Oliver Cromwell, Absalom with the Duke of Monmouth, Achitophel with Shaftesbury, and Zimri with Buckingham. He would have been a dull-witted reader, who missed the implied references to Charles II in the opening lines, to Cromwell and his son and the restored monarch in the body of the poem :

> They who when Saul was dead, without a blow
> Made foolish Ishbosheth the crown forego;
> Who banished David did from Hebron bring,
> And with a general shout proclaimed him king,

or to the Duke of Monmouth, Buckingham, and Shaftesbury in the full-length portraits. The political situation was a stern actuality in men's minds, and a serious purpose possesses the poem. The *Medal* (1682), ikewise an occasional poem, contains obvious references o the temporary triumph of Shaftesbury and to the honour bestowed upon him :

> The word pronounced aloud by shrieval voice
> Laetamur, which in Polish is rejoice.

But in *MacFlecknoe* (1682) Dryden was concerned with a literary enemy, and, thereby, anticipated Pope. The *Medal* had produced several retorts, among which the *Medal of John Bayes*, by his old friend, Shadwell, gave Dryden most annoyance. Piqued by the revival of the old controversy inaugurated in the *Rehearsal* (1681) and by the strictures on his recent political satire, Dryden turned upon Shadwell the full measure of his wrath, superficial resemblances between Shadwell and Flecknoe being maliciously seized upon. Marvell had already composed a satirical poem on this ill-starred poetaster, whose alleged reason for writing was " chiefly to avoid idleness." " I print to avoid the imputation [of idleness] and as others do it to live after they are dead, I do it only not to be thought dead whilst I am alive." Occasional signs of talent had, indeed, appeared in Flecknoe, but the satirist fell foul of him, and no compliment could be implied in the portrait. Unlike the political and personal satires, the *Religio Laici* (1682) and the *Hind and the Panther* (1687) indicate the poet's theological position, his faith in the English establishment, and, after his change of front, in the Church of Rome. Here, the matter is argumentative and didactic, a triumph of reasoning in verse.

It is in this group of political, satirical, and theological poems that Dryden attained to his highest achievement. It will be well to have done, at once, with strictures. Dryden's satire degenerates here and there into mere brutality, in the reference, for example, to Shaftesbury's son :

> And all to leave what with his toil he won
> To that unfeathered two-legged thing, a son
> Got, while his soul did huddled notions try,
> And born, a shapeless lump, like anarchy,

sometimes into irreverence, as in the passage on Nadab (Lord Howard of Escrick). *MacFlecknoe* is disfigured by much of that coarseness which satirists are wont to admit into their verses. Again, the didactic *Hind and the Panther* rests on a conception which, as Johnson remarked, is " both injudicious and incommodious." " What," he asks, " can be more absurd than that one beast should counsel another to rest her faith upon a pope and council ? ", and Dryden's fable lent itself to easy ridicule in Prior's travesty. But the merits may easily be understated. Compared with Pope's, Dryden's satire rarely takes undue advantage. He can be coarse and virulent, but he displays his colours, without stooping to " hint a fault and hesitate dislike." Pope could sneer at poverty, Dryden was concerned,

first and foremost, with character. It is this which
has made justly famous his full-length portraits of
Achitophel (Shaftesbury), Zimri (Buckingham), Shimei
(Slingsby Bethel), Corah (Titus Oates), Barzillai (Duke
of Ormond), and Shadwell—the progressive character
of which Coleridge noted :

> Take Dryden's Achitophel and Zimri; every line adds to or
> modifies the character, which is, as it were, a-building up to the
> very last verse; whereas in Pope's Timon, etc., the first two or three
> couplets contain all the pith of the character, and the twenty or
> thirty lines that follow are so much evidence or proof of overt acts
> of jealousy, or pride, or whatever it may be that is satirized.

From the standpoint of diction and versification, no
praise of these poems can be too high. The metre
represents a return to the heroic couplet and a final
abandonment of the stanza of *Annus Mirabilis*. It
would be difficult to estimate to what extent Dryden's
adoption of this verse-form influenced poets of the
eighteenth century. But his couplet is not to be con-
founded with Pope's or even Waller's, and Dryden's
position in the seventeenth century is comparable with
that of Marlowe in the sixteenth. The characteristics
of his line are vigour and rapidity, rather than studied
elegance. His is the " mighty line " once more, and,
if Waller was smooth,

> Dryden taught to join
> The varying verse, the full-resounding line,
> The long majestic march, and energy divine.

Other characteristics differentiate Dryden's versification
from that of the rigid-couplet exponents. Not only is
his individual line more masculine and his diction
less reminiscent of Parnassus, but he permits him-
self freedom with the cæsura, triple rhymes, and
alexandrines—no doubt, from a conviction that for
narrative purposes some less resticted medium was
essential.

If we consider how much more Dryden produced,
whether in lyric, ode, or couplet, we shall not be inclined

to accuse him of fastidiousness. His output was astounding in both quality and quantity, and he depended less upon a few measures than might be supposed. The couplet was his maid-of-all-work, employed not only for satire and theology, but in his renderings of Virgil and Juvenal. He experimented in other metres in the magnificent hymn, *Veni Creator* (octosyllabic), and the lyrics, while his mastery over the English form of ode is apparent in the two examples, written in honour of St. Cecilia's Day and in the lines to Anne Killigrew, where he is the peer of Cowley, the founder of the measure. Dryden is assuredly worthy of the tribute which Johnson, in summing up his achievement, bestowed upon him : " What was said of Rome, adorned by Augustus, may be applied by an easy metaphor to English poetry, embellished by Dryden, *lateritiam invenit, marmoream reliquit* : ' He found it brick and he left it marble.' "

II. NON-DRAMATIC CRITICISM

During the decade 1680-90, Dryden was mainly occupied with satire and light verse; the last ten years of his life he devoted to translation and criticism, supplementing his earlier version of Ovid (1680) and extending the range of his critical work. The latter, now applied exclusively to the non-dramatic field, exemplifies in a remarkable way that command over " the other harmony of prose," which, with his achievement in verse, constitutes Dryden the typical man-of-letters. The *Discourse Concerning the Original and Progress of Satire* (1693) which accompanied the translation of Juvenal owed its outline to Dacier. But Dryden is sufficiently original in his estimates of Horace, Persius, and Juvenal, and we could ill spare the modern references—to Spenser, Shakespeare, and Jonson. Dryden becomes more intimate in speaking of writers he knew—of Milton,

who is flat only when he "is got into a track of
scripture," Donne, who "affects the metaphysics,"
and Cowley, "the darling of my youth," and there is
high praise for "the admirable Boileau." Numerous
personal touches enliven the pages : "More libels have
been written against me, than almost any man now
living : and I had reason on my side, to have defended
my own innocence "; and there is a reference to " a slip
of an old man's memory " to explain an oversight in
connexion with *Hudibras*. Dryden returns again to the
subject of the heroic poem, briefly expounds his theory
of translation, and hints that he has in mind a history
of English prosody. The *Parallel Between Poetry and
Painting* (1695), a translation of Du Fresnoy's *De Arte
Graphica*, was published in 1668, together with a French
version. In the opening pages, Dryden quotes at length
from Bellori's *Lives of the Painters, Sculptors*, etc.
(1672), associating himself with its idealistic standpoint :
" The business of his preface is to prove that a learned
painter should form to himself an idea of perfect
Nature. This image he is to set before his mind in all
his undertakings, and to draw from thence, as from a
store-house, the beauties which are to enter into his
work ; there correcting Nature from what actually she is
in individuals, to what she ought to be, and what she
was created." Later, in commenting upon Du Fresnoy
himself, Dryden wrote : "This is notoriously true in
these two arts; for the way to please being to imitate
Nature, both the poets and the painters, in ancient
times and in the best ages, have studied her ; and from
the practice of both these arts the rules have been drawn
by which we are instructed how to please, and to
compass that end which they obtained, by following
their example. For Nature is still the same in all ages,
and can never be contrary to herself." The importance
of all this in connexion with the Augustan doctrine of
" nature " cannot be overlooked. Sir Joshua Reynolds
knew Du Fresnoy's book, and in his *Discourses* cited

with approval his comparison of the painter's colouring to *lena sororis*, "that which procures lovers and admirers to the more valuable excellences of the art," though he failed to agree with either the author or Dryden that "the principal figure of a subject must appear in the midst of the picture, under the principal light, to distinguish it from the rest," calling attention to the technique of Le Brun's *Tent of Darius*, among other pictures.

The critical masterpiece of the period was, however, the *Preface to the Fables* (1700), composed within a few months of Dryden's death. Here all is original and the essay is worthy to be set, side by side, with the earlier one on dramatic poetry. Versions of the first book of the *Iliad*, parts of the *Metamorphoses*, of Chaucer and Boccaccio accompany the essay. Beginning with his reasons for associating Chaucer and Boccaccio, Dryden passes to a comparison between Homer and Virgil: "Homer's invention was more copious, Virgil's more confined; so that if Homer had not led the way, it was not in Virgil to have begun heroic poetry; for nothing can be more evident than that the Roman poem is but the second part of the Ilias; a continuation of the same story, and the persons already formed. . . . The very heroes show their authors; Achilles is hot, impatient, revengeful—

> Impiger, iracundus, inexorabilis, acer, etc.,

Æneas patient, considerate, careful of his people, and merciful to his enemies; ever submissive to the will of Heaven—

> . . . quo fata trahunt, retrahuntque sequamur."

Then follows the more important part of the essay—the lengthy comparison between Ovid and Chaucer—which definitely proves Dryden's side in the controversy between ancients and moderns. Chaucer is honoured as the father of English poetry, and praised as a "perpetual fountain of good sense," who follows

Nature everywhere and " has taken into the compass of his *Canterbury Tales* the various manners and humours (as we now call them) of the whole English nation, in his age. . . . 'Tis sufficient to say, according to the proverb, that *here is God's plenty*." But Chaucer's language and metre prove a stumbling-block. The former Dryden gives up " as a post not to be defended in our poet, because he wanted the modern art of fortifying." As for the metre, he cannot agree with Speght that " the fault is in our ears, and that there were really ten syllables in a verse where we find but nine." Consequently, he declares that he will not confine himself to a literal translation. The key to his modernizations is to be found, however, in that theory of translation, which he set forth in the Preface to the translation of Ovid's *Epistles* (1680). Since the Renaissance, two views of the translator's office had been commonly held. On the one hand, men like Jonson and Marvell had clung to the theory of literal translation; compare Marvell's poetical address to his friend, Dr. Witty :

> Others do strive with words and forced phrase
> To add such lustre, and so many rays,
> That but to make the vessel shining, they
> Much of the precious metal rub away.
> He is translation's thief that addeth more,
> As much as he that taketh from the store
> Of the first author.

Others, like Sibilet in France and Denham in England, holding that the translator's function was the enrichment of the vernacular by conveying ancient ideas into modern moulds, declined the servile path of " tracing word by word and line by line." Dryden's view was in accord with Denham's, for while he recognized three methods of translation—*metaphrase*, or " turning an author word by word and line by line from one language into another " ; *paraphrase,* or " translation with latitude, where the author is kept in view by the translator, so as never to be lost, but his words are not so strictly followed as his sense "; and *imitation*, " where the translator (if now he has not lost that name) assumes the liberty, not only to vary from the words and sense, but to forsake them both as he sees occasion; and taking only some general hints from the original, to run division on the ground-work, as he pleases "—his own preference was for the second of these methods.

When Dryden came to apply his principles to Chaucer he recognized, however, that his version would scarcely please the Saxon enthusiasts—men like Hickes, Hearne, and Rymer—since, in accordance with Restoration theory, the work must needs be adapted to his own age, the diction " fortified," the metre polished, and the manners " corrected." The " workman's skill " must be in evidence, for

> by improving what was writ before,
> Invention labours less, but judgment more.
> —Roscommon: *Essay on Translated Verse.*

Dryden, accordingly, modified the versification by the employment of triplets and alexandrines, ousted a number of obsolete words, and polished generally. In *Palamon and Arcite*, contemporary taste appears, at the outset, in the antithetical description of the Scythian queen,

> Whom first by force he conquered, then by love;

in the mythological reference,

> Aurora had but newly chased the night,
> And purpled o'er the sky with blushing light,

and the Parnassus epithet " fatal dart." There is, besides, an avoidance of illustrations, either too familiar or naïve, with the result that Chaucer's couplet

> His slepy yerde in hond he bar uprighte,
> An hat he werede upon his heres brighte,

becomes

> His hat adorned with wings disclosed the god,
> And in his hand he bore the sleep-compelling rod.

But it may be doubted whether Dryden has
" improved " the following lines

> And over al this, to sleen me utterly,
> Love hath his fyry dart so brenningly
> Y-stiked thurgh my trewe careful herte,
> That shapen was my deeth erst than my sherte.
> Ye sleen me with your eyen, Emelye;
> Ye been the cause wherfor that I dye,

by substituting

> But love's a malady without a cure:
> Fierce Love has pierced me with his fiery dart,
> He fries within, and hisses at my heart.
> Your eyes, fair Emily, my fate pursue;
> I suffer for the rest, I die for you.

Yet Dryden always had an eye in his adaptations for
Chaucer's great effects :

> For with the rosy colour strove her hue,

or

> The morning-lark, the messenger of day,
> Saluteth in her song the morning gray;
> And soon the sun arose with beams so bright,
> That all the horizon laughed to see the joyous sight,

and, in the following, achieved a triumph of his own :

> Not Juno moves with more majestic grace,
> And all the Cyprian queen is in her face.

VI

FIELDING'S VOYAGE TO LISBON

AMONG that curious series of autobiographical productions in English literature, most familiarly represented by the diaries of Evelyn and Pepys, the *Journal to Stella*, and the memoirs of Gibbon and Miss Burney, few have more sustained interest than the remarkable *Journal of a Voyage to Lisbon* by Henry Fielding, Esq., Justice of the Peace for Middlesex and Westminster. Infinitely less valuable in its bearing on social questions than the gossipy shorthand notes of Pepys, it has still a claim upon the historian of the eighteenth century, and in purely personal interest remains unsurpassed for mingled humour and tenderness. In the history of Fielding's life, the *Journal* fills a gap which could never have been satisfactorily understood otherwise, and his biographers from Murphy downwards have given the close of his career in a mere transcript of Fielding's own notes on the voyage.

"Our immortal Fielding," though posterity has thrown doubts on this statement of Gibbon's, "was of the younger branch of the Earls of Denbigh, who drew their origin from the Counts of Hapsburgh." Born in 1707, he received his early education at the hands of a Mr. Oliver, the family chaplain, was early removed to Eton, and finally proceeded to the University of Leyden. At the end of a two years' course, Fielding became aware that his remittances were growing "small by degrees and beautifully less," and, when at length they ceased altogether, he reluctantly returned to London. Thrown without warning upon his own resources, he turned to the stage for a livelihood, and, during the next few years, lived entirely upon his plays. But the passing of the *Licensing Act* in 1739 compelled him to turn elsewhere—to law and journalism. The literary history of Fielding is his history as a novelist, and, by his original work in fiction from *Joseph Andrews* (1742) to *Amelia* (1751), he has earned a foremost position among English men-of-letters. From the date of his first novel to his death in 1754, Fielding's life was devoted to his profession as a barrister and to literary work. In 1748 he had been appointed Justice of the Peace for Middlesex and Westminster, and was continuously occupied with the magisterial duties appertaining thereto. The office of a paid Middlesex magistrate was not held in very high estimation, being regarded generally as a mere trading post, in which officials practised a rigorous system of exaction. Yet the manner, in which the novelist performed his duties, seems to have given much satisfaction, and though his private life was censured by the fastidious Walpole, he attaches no severer stigma to his character than that he banquetted with a blind man off cold mutton and the bone of a ham.

By the close of 1752 Fielding had taken final leave of fiction. His financial affairs at this date were not entirely satisfactory, and, in defending himself against the charge of seeking personal preferment in his scheme for the relief of the poor, he wrote : " Ambition or avarice can no longer raise a hope or dictate any scheme to me, who have no further design than to pass my short remainder of life in some degree of ease, and barely to preserve my family from being the objects of any such laws as I have here proposed." From this point onwards, Fielding gives us a detailed account of his career in what Austin Dobson has described as " one of the most unfeigned and touching little tracts in English literature." An *Introduction to the Journal*, probably added in Lisbon, explains the circumstances leading up to the voyage, and Fielding's editors have been relieved from surmises as to the actual course of events. By this date (1753) (we have merely to draw upon the *Introduction* for our information), Fielding's health seems to have broken down, and he was regularly taking the Duke of Portland's medicine—a specific against the gout. A slight improvement resulting upon this, he was advised to go to Bath, the fashionable resort for invalids. Within a few days of his setting out, he received a note ordering his immediate attendance upon the Duke of Newcastle. He waited on his Grace, found him particularly engaged, was meantime interviewed by a gentleman upon the question of the recent robberies in London, and, finally, after an interval of a few days, undertook the drawing up of a scheme for the suppression of the aforesaid nuisances. In consequence of this commission, Fielding was kept in town throughout the severe winter of 1753, though at the time " in a deep jaundice," and it was only in the following spring, after seeing his schemes successful and the hooligans dispersed, that he was able to escape to the country, according to his own account, " in a very weak and deplorable condition, with no fewer or less diseases than a jaundice, a dropsy, and an asthma."

Fielding's case was no longer a " Bath case," and in February he consulted Ward, the noted quack, best known from Pope's line as trying " on Puppies and the Poor his drop." The treatment seems to have been of some avail, and the novelist experienced an improvement in health. A perusal of Berkeley's *Siris*, a philosophical treatise in which the virtues of tar-water as a panacea are extolled in audacious flights of language, induced him to adopt yet a third mode of treatment. As a consequence, his condition further improved, and, in the strength of revived spirits, he decided to avoid the experiences of the former winter by taking a voyage to Lisbon.

In considering the *Journal of a Voyage to Lisbon,*

it is necessary to remember that it was written for publication. The three parts of which it consists are distinct. The printer's dedication is hardly more than a plea for leniency on the part of the reader towards any failings revealed in the work, with the additional statement that the material has been presented to the public " as it came from the hands of the author." Despite this, there are reasons for believing that the edition of 1755 underwent considerable " editing." Mrs. Francis becomes Mrs. Humphreys, and particulars of the visit to Newcastle are omitted. The name of the Captain, suppressed in the *Journal*, may be found in Fielding's last letter, written to his brother and headed : " On board the Queen of Portugal, Rich^d. Veal, at anchor on the Mother Bank off Ryde," July 12th, 1754.

As for the author's preface, this treats mainly of the function of the adventure-writer, buttressing itself on the authority of Horace, and is important for the evidence it contains as to the ulterior purpose of the *Journal*. It approaches its theme in a spirit arising from a sense of novelty, and one is reminded of the prefaces which ushered the two great novels into the world. As in the introduction to *Joseph Andrews*, Fielding enumerates his predecessors in this particular style of composition, and it is interesting to observe how his naturally critical instinct forces him to the conclusion that Addison, as a writer of travel, remained a mere commentator on the classics. Of voyage-narrative, in general, he attempts no definition, and is thus saved from incurring the censure of those who object to his definition of the novel as a comic epic in prose. Yet, with the over-zeal of one who applies all his energies to the work in hand, Fielding ventures into an invidious comparison between fiction and fact. " I must confess," he says, " I should have honoured and loved Homer more had he written a true history of his own times in humble prose, than those noble poems that have so justly collected the praise of all ages; for though I read these with more admiration and astonishment, I still read Herodotus, Thucydides and Xenophon with more amusement and more satisfaction." The reader of *Joseph Andrews* may be inclined to doubt the sincerity of this, and would rather believe that he is here putting up a case for his new venture in autobiography. In a later passage, Fielding writes: " It is sufficient that every fact should have its foundation in truth "—a remark which may be taken as a defence of Homer and an indication that the author has allowed his imagination free course.

The interest of this little posthumous work lies, mainly, in its intimate character. The events which brought Fielding's life to a close, with the exception of the last two months at Lisbon, are rehearsed in detail, and, throughout the entries, a tenderness is exhibited such as will puzzle the reader, who, with Mr. Edwards of Turrick, still labours under the conviction that " the fellow had no heart." Fielding, whose early career has so often perturbed the propriety of readers, lies within exposed to the critical eye. Yet the man who hands down to posterity a picture of his wife as " the tenderest mother in the world," who repels the applauses of his friends, " to which I well knew I had no title," and, of the Captain imploring mercy on his knees, writes: " I did not suffer a brave man and an old man to remain a moment in this posture; but immediately forgave him," was surely no stranger to tenderness, nor a character altogether unlovable.

Beyond this personal element, the genius which made Fielding pre-eminent as a novelist is conspicuous throughout. Of the character-sketches, scattered here and there, no two opinions can be held. The genius of the novelist shows no signs of faltering in the portraits of the Captain and Mrs. Francis, the former of which is a masterpiece, with all the appearance of a sketch from the life. Veal is no blusterer unredeemed by humane touches, no mere lay-figure, such as

characterizes the pictorial art of Smollett : " He wore
a sword of no ordinary length by his side, with which
he swaggered in his cabin, among the wretches his
passengers, whom he had stowed in cupboards on each
side," yet, in contrast to this petty tyranny, we find
him later " acting the part of a father to his sailors,
and even extending humanity to animals."

Veal's truculence is illustrated in the scene, which
Fielding, refusing to be dominated, brings to a termina-
tion by violently threatening his " polyonymous officer "
(" captain's valet-de-chambre, head cook, house and ship
steward, footman in livery and out on't, secretary and
fore-mast man "), while his softer side is effectively
revealed in the story of the drowning kitten : " The
captain's humanity, if I may so call it, did not so totally
destroy his philosophy as to make him yield himself
up to affliction on this melancholy occasion. Having
felt his loss like a man, he resolved to show he could
bear it like one; and, having declared he had rather
have lost a cask of rum or brandy, betook himself to
threshing at backgammon with the Portuguese friar,
in which innocent amusement they had passed about
two-thirds of their time." Then there is Mrs. Francis,
in some respects even better than Veal : " She was a
short, squat woman; her head was closely joined to her
shoulders, where it was fixed somewhat awry; every
feature of her countenance was sharp and pointed; her
face was furrowed with the smallpox; and her com-
plexion, which seemed to be able to turn milk to curds,
not a little resembled in colour such milk as had already
undergone that operation." This lady distinguished
herself, in her relationships with Fielding, by her
rapacity : " If her bills were remonstrated against she
was offended with the tacit censure of her fair-dealing;
if they were not she seemed to regard it as a tacit sarcasm
on her folly, which might have set down larger prices
with the same success." The minor characters are the
customs officer, whose conduct led Fielding to conclude

that State officials " seem industriously picked out of
the lowest and vilest orders of mankind," the young
military fellow, nephew to the Captain, who hated all
fools, and a type of the average stage-coachman of the
eighteenth century.

In these portraits, humour is the predominating
feature, and we are frequently reminded of Dickens.
To one unacquainted with Fielding, reading the *Journal*
for the first time, his irony is often a pitfall. A sentence
opens in the gravest manner, the reader following gaily,
heedless of danger, until at the climax he realizes the
snare into which he has fallen. Only after several such
surprises does he become chary enough to turn the
tables on himself by presupposing dangers which never
existed. Of less disguised flashes there are innumerable
examples, combined, on occasion, with a vivid realism,
as in the departure-scene at Wapping: " Besides the dis-
agreeable situation in which we then lay, in the confines
of Wapping and Rotherhithe, tasting a delicious mixture
of the air of both these sweet places, and enjoying the
concord of sweet sounds of seamen, watermen, fish-
women, oyster-women, and of all the vociferous
inhabitants of both shores, composing altogether a
greater variety of harmony than Hogarth's imagination
hath brought together in that print of his, which is
enough to make a man deaf to look at—I had a more
urgent cause to press our departure . . ." or, again,
with witty application of his Latin, the account of the
landing at Ryde: " I was pretty easily conveyed on
board this hoy; but to get from hence to the shore was
not so easy a task; for, however strange it may appear,
the water itself did not extend so far; an instance which
seems to explain those lines of Ovid,

Omnia pontus erant, deerant quoque littora ponto,

in a less tautological sense than hath generally been
imputed to them." Confronted with the two kinds of
travel, by land and by sea, Fielding decides to confine
himself to the latter, declaring, with painful reminis-

cence, that "whatever is said on this subject is applicable to both alike, and we may bring them together as closely as they are brought in the liturgy, where they are recommended to the prayers of all Christian congregations; and (which I have often thought very remarkable) where they are joined with the miserable wretches, such as people in sickness, infants just born, prisoners and captives." Again, the state-room in which he slept is described as "a most stately apartment, capable of containing one human body in length, if not very tall, and three bodies in breadth."

Throughout the voyage Fielding retains his magisterial eye, interspersing lengthy reflections on the condition of the English navy, the value of fish as a staple commodity, the characteristics of English sailors, the general system of quarantine in Lisbon, and other topics innumerable.

In a work of this description, consisting of mere daily records, the author is relieved of regular method, and no kind of architectonic structure need be expected. Yet, in point of style, the *Journal* exhibits Fielding at his best, the chief defect of the novels, absence of clause-architecture, being less apparent. The short, crisp sentence frequently appears, and, where colons or semicolons take the place of the stop, each division may be regarded as representing a logical unit. Occasionally, Fielding is clumsy and obscure, but instances are rare.

The following will serve as an example : "He said, indeed, more to my wife, and used more rhetoric to dissuade her from having it drawn than is generally employed to persuade young ladies to prefer a pain of three moments to one of three months' continuance, especially if those young ladies happen to be past forty and fifty years of age, when, by submitting to support a racking torment, the only good circumstance attending which is, it is so short that scarce one in a thousand can cry out : ' I feel it,' they are to do a violence to their charms, and lose one of those beautiful holders with which alone Sir Courtly Nice declares a lady can ever lay hold of his heart."

In conclusion, the *Journal of a Voyage to Lisbon* is chiefly valuable for the view it presents of Fielding's character. " If any portrait of the novelist," says Austin Dobson, " is to be handed down, let it be—not the Fielding of the green-room and the tavern, of Covent Garden frolics and modern conversations, but the energetic magistrate, the tender husband and father, the kind host of his poorer friends, the practical philanthropist, the patient, magnanimous hero of the *Voyage to Lisbon*."

VII

PRECURSORS OF THE ROMANTIC REVIVAL

I. THE FIRST PHASE AND THE MOVEMENT IN THE NORTH

THE age of classicism in England was not precisely co-extensive with the eighteenth century. The Augustan age remained the classic age *par excellence*, but with the supremacy of Johnson there were clear signs of a revolt. Yet, from 1698-1798, the classic note pre-dominated, and is nowhere more clearly evidenced than in the attitude towards Nature of writers at opposite extremes of the century. Pope's *Windsor Forest* reveals no deep appreciation of natural scenery, while Johnson's preference for Fleet Street to the Hebrides is notorious. It was Johnson, again, who described a Highland peak as " a considerable protuberance," while Gibbon spoke of Caledonia as a region of " gloomy hills assailed by the winter tempest, lakes concealed in blue mist, and cold and lonely heaths over which the deer of the forest were chased by a troop of naked barbarians."

In his *Crotchet Castle* Peacock has cleverly defined the characteristics of what he called the " civic poet ": " The cowslip of a civic poet is always in blossom, his fern is always in full feather, he gathers the celandine, the primrose, the heathflower, the jasmine and the chrysanthemum always on the same day and from the same spot; his nightingale sings all the year round, his moon is always full, his cygnet is as white as his swan, his cedar is as tremulous as his aspen, and his poplar as embowering as his beech. It is an age of liberality, indeed, when not to know an oak from a

burdock is no disqualification for sylvan minstrelsy."
This may well be contrasted with the Shakespearian
method, exemplified in the flower-scene in the *Winter's
Tale*, with its ordered catalogue of autumn, summer, and
spring flowers.

Though the pseudo-classic style, with its contempt
for the exotic and the antique, dominated the eighteenth
century, it is a commonplace that traces of the new
movement appear, here and there, throughout the
century, alike in verse and in the new theories of land-
scape-gardening. The revolt in the direction of
romanticism began in England with Anne, Countess of
Winchelsea, who died in 1720. A special interest
attaches to her name from a passage in Wordsworth's
Preface to the *Lyrical Ballads*, in which, with some
exaggeration, he declared that " excepting the *Nocturnal
Reverie* and a passage or two in the *Windsor Forest* of
Pope, the poetry of the period intervening between the
publication of *Paradise Lost* and the *Seasons* does not
contain a single new image of external nature." The
Countess's *Nocturnal Reverie* is a compendium of things
seen : " the waving moon " amid " the trembling
leaves," " the cool bank whence springs the woodbine
and the bramble rose," " the foxglove " of " paler hue,"
yet chequering still " with red the dusky brakes," and
the remarkable picture of the loosed horse " slowly
grazing through the adjoining meads, whose stealing
pace and lengthened shade we fear, till torn-up forage
in his teeth we hear."

This represents the simplest aspect of romanticism—
the return to nature. The undue depreciation into
which the term has fallen is due in part to a reaction
against the heterodoxy of Rousseau, but there can be
no doubt that it supplies a convenient formula for
expressing that particular aspect of the new movement,
the love of open-air scenery, which was to culminate
in the nature-worship of Wordsworth and the Lakists.

Of the new nature-school the real head was James

Thomson, one of that line of Scotchmen, to whom English literature owes so much, and the most original figure between Pope and Gray. The *Seasons* came out sectionally, the first instalment appearing in 1726 under the title *Winter*, followed by *Summer* in 1727, *Spring* (1728), and the completed volume in 1730. Thomson was essentially a realist. If we compare the attitude of the civic poet as described by Peacock with Thomson's catalogue of spring flowers, we cannot fail to be struck by the change now inaugurated :

> In yon mingled wilderness of flowers.
> Fair-handed Spring unbosoms every grace;
> Throws out the snow-drop and the crocus first:
> The daisy, primrose, violet darkly blue,
> And polyanthus of unnumbered dyes:
> The yellow wallflower stained with iron-brown.

Rustic and nature scenes abound in the *Seasons*, together with miniature pictorial effects, dashed off from the poet's pen. There is the rainbow " refracted from yon eastern cloud, bestriding earth in fair proportion, running from the red to where the violet fades into the sky," the house-dog lying " with the vacant greyhound, outstretched and sleepy," the spider sitting " in eager watch amid a mangled heap of carcases."   In these rustic sketches, Thomson succeeds perhaps better than in such literary episodes as those of Celadon and Amelia and Damon and Musidora.

The *Castle of Indolence* (1748), Thomson's second contribution to the literature of romance, was a figment of the poet's brain, conceived in dream-imagery and shrouded in an opiate atmosphere. The charm of the metre—the Spenserian stanza—and the diction set the *Castle of Indolence* in the direct ancestry of the great dream-poems, the *Revolt of Islam* and the *Lotos-Eaters* :

> A pleasing land of drowsy-head it was,
>   Of dreams that wave before the half-shut eye;
> And of gay castles in the clouds that pass,
>   For ever flushing round a summer sky:
> There eke the soft delights, that witchingly

> Instil a wanton sweetness through the breast;
> And the calm pleasures always hovered nigh;
> But whate'er smacked of noyance or unrest,
> Was far, far off expelled from this delicious nest.

Thomson cannot altogether free himself from the conventions of eighteenth century diction. He is one of the greatest defaulters in the use of periphrases, " plumy people " for birds, " brittle bondage " for an egg-shell, etc., and occasionally employs a pompous Latinized diction, for which his model was Milton. Of this, the most amusing example is the oft-quoted " sportive lambs, this way and that, convolved in friskful glee."

In the wake of Thomson came " Matthew Green, who wrote the *Spleen*," and John Dyer of *Grongar Hill*. A natural and genial poet, Green attempted a medical theme in light octosyllabic verse. The introduction of new verse-forms at a time when the heroic couplet held paramount position is worthy of note. Both Green and Dyer wrote in ,octosyllables, Thomson, Young, and Blair in blank verse, while the *Castle of Indolence* and Shenstone's *Schoolmistress* revived the Spenserian stanza.

Dyer's *Grongar Hill* (1727) stands out as a rarity in a barren age, with a refreshing and novel metre. It is the verse of *L'Allegro*, with, on the whole, a graver movement. The following lines illustrate Dyer's characteristic charm :

> Now, ev'n now, my joys run high,
> As on the mountain turf I lie;
> While the wanton Zephyr sings,
> And in the vale perfumes his wings;
> While the waters murmur deep;
> While the shepherd charms his sheep;
> While the birds unbounded fly,
> And with musick fill the sky,
> Now, ev'n now, my joys run high.

To poetry Dyer brought the experience of a trained artist, who had rambled far and wide, portfolio under arm. Of the early school of English water-colourists, he won the praise of Wordsworth, and to him we owe the graphic description of Sarum plain " spread like Ocean's boundless round, where solitary Stonehenge, grey with moss, ruin of ages nods." Later in the century, in another medium, this enthusiasm is reflected in the novel ideas of landscape-gardening put forward by Whately in his *Observations on Modern Gardening* (1770) and Gilpin in his *Observations on the River Wye,* etc. (1782).

Young and Blair, the poets of night and the grave, contributed less to the movement than some of their less-gifted contemporaries. In their use of blank verse they were of the school of Thomson, and indulge in a pomposity of style and a fuliginous splendour in keeping with their themes. Young's *Night Thoughts* was highly popular in its day, and won the admiration of Klopstock, Diderot, and the French romantics. Blair's is the best of eighteenth century mortuary poems, and rises superior to its companion, but both have a claim to be included here, if only for their eeriness and solemnity.

The Spenserian stanza, employed in the *Castle of Indolence,* reappeared in Shenstone's *Schoolmistress* (1737), a happy burlesque of scenes in rural life. Shenstone applied his landscape skill in other directions, and gained notoriety by the artistic methods he applied to his land and gardens. His sober descriptions are in strong contrast with the crude effects of a writer like Savage.

The school of Thomson culminated in Gray and Collins. The cause of the former was ardently championed by Sir Edmund Gosse, while Swinburne said the final word in appreciation of Collins: " As an elegiac poet, Gray holds for all ages to come his unassailable and sovereign station : as a lyric poet he is simply unworthy to sit at the feet of Collins." Swinburne's staunch advocacy was, perhaps, not altogether unbiassed by the fact that Collins was among the first to sound the trumpet of republican faith, but the dictum is right, in the main. In the history of romanticism Gray, however, holds a unique place by his introduction of themes from the Norse. P. H. Mallet's *Introduction à l'Histoire de Dannemarc* had appeared in 1755, and with this Gray was familiar. His *Fatal Sisters* was a paraphrase from Torfæus (1697), the original being an Icelandic court-poem of *c.* 1028, entitled the *Lay of Darts*, while the source of the *Descent of Odin* may be found in the *Elder Edda*. Collins, on the other hand, was of the school of landscape painters and, in this respect, a successor of Dyer. "Corot on canvas," says Swinburne, "might have signed Collins's *Ode to Evening*." Gray's contributions to the history of romanticism were not, however, confined to translations from the Norse. Admittedly a sterile poet, he fell upon an age of prose, and, as Matthew Arnold expressed it, "never spake out." But Gray had sensibility enough to justify a larger output, and the paucity of his actual production remains a problem. Possibly the conditions under which he lived may be adduced in partial explanation. A Cambridge don of fastidious temperament, a scholarly recluse and voluminous reader, Gray did not readily yield to the impulse to print. He lacked, besides, the incentive which might have roused a poorer man. Still, within the limits of his actual verse-production, Gray has left remarkable anticipations of the future directions of romanticism. It has sometimes been overlooked that there is, in the *Elegy* itself, a distinctly romantic note : its tenderness and humanity constitute it a portion of that "poetry of the heart," which romanticism claims as its own. Standing between two ages, the *Elegy* looks backward to Dante and Petrarch and the Elizabethans, yet forward to Wordsworth. Equally remarkable are the lines in the *Sonnet on the Death of Richard West* and the *Ode on the Pleasure Arising from Vicissitude* :

> Till April starts, and calls around
> The sleeping fragrance from the ground,
> And lightly o'er the living scene
> Scatters her freshest, tenderest green,
>
> *(Vicissitude,* 12-15)

together with the Wordsworthian anticipation :

> The meanest flowret of the vale,
> The simplest note that swells the gale,
> The common sun, the air, the skies,
> To him are opening Paradise.
>
> *(Ibid.,* 49-52.)

Johnson was severe on the sequestered virtues of Gray, but was debarred from full acquaintance with one side of his achievement, familiar to modern readers in the *Letters.* These reveal him in many aspects— sprightly, gay, humorous, artistic, and romantic. From Bologna he sends an enthusiastic description of the picture-galleries at Parma (December 9th, 1739), describes the Good Friday celebrations at Rome (April 15th, 1740), writes a humorous account of his experiences in the style of Swift (Spring, 1740), and indulges his taste for classical atmosphere in the description of a visit to Alba (May, 1740). With all this, the *Letters* provide the first adequate examples of romantic nature-description. The letter to Richard West (November, 1739) contains the rhapsodic account of the Grande Chartreuse : " Not a precipice, not a torrent, not a cliff, but is pregnant with religion and poetry. There are certain scenes that would awe an atheist into belief, without the help of other argument," while the journal of the *Tour in the Lakes* speaks enthusiastically of the " turbulent chaos " of mountains round Borrowdale and of " the solemn colouring of light " on Derwentwater. Further, there is in the *Letters* more than one contribution to the calendar of the seasons, worthy of the century of Gilbert White, e.g. : " I observed, that on December 2, many of our Rose-trees had put out new leaves, and the Lauristine, Polyanthus, single yellow, and bloody Wall-flowers, Cytisus, and scarlet Geraniums were still in flower " (January 31st, 1761), or, again : " Currants begun to ripen on the 8th, and red gooseberries had changed colour; tares were then in flower, and meadow-hay cutting. Lime-trees in full bloom on the 9th. Mushrooms in perfection on the 17th " (July 21st, 1759).

Writing to Horace Walpole from Cambridge in October, 1751, Gray remarked : " We have a man here that writes a good hand; but he has little failings that hinder my recommending him to you. He is lousy, and he is mad : he sets out this week for Bedlam; but if you insist upon it, I don't doubt he will pay his respects to you." So much for Christopher Smart, whose master-piece, the *Song to David*, appeared in print twelve years later—a fervent Biblical poem, exaggerated and even grotesque, yet, by its inspiration, its sweep and vigour, one of the triumphant achievements of its age.

Meantime, poetry had taken a somewhat different course in the north. The history of Lowland Scottish literature—the lineal descendant of Old Northumbrian—is an integral part of the history of English literature, in general. In the somewhat arid period of the fifteenth century, the tradition of Chaucer had been maintained by a noble band north of the Tweed, and, during the classic period of Pope and the Augustans, the new romantic movement began under the leadership of Allan Ramsay, the Edinburgh wig-maker. Though Ramsay earned for himself an assured position in Scottish literature as independent man-of-letters, and is widely known by his songs, *Auld Lang Syne* and *Lochaber No More* from the *Tea-Table Miscellany* (1724-7), it was as collector and editor of ballads in the *Evergreen* (1724) that he most directly influenced the new movement. For whereas the particular direction of romanticism in the south lay in a revived interest in nature, in the north the movement was characterized by a renewed use of the vernacular and traditional ballad-literature. The long line of collectors, with Ramsay at their head, form important landmarks in the history of the century. David Herd, James Johnson, Pinkerton, Ritson, each of these holds an independent position either as editor or adapter of traditional ballads, their work culminating in the monumental collections of Scott and Jamieson. The origin and nature of ballads is one of the problems of literary history. On the one hand, folk-lorists deny that they are the product of a special literary class, and seek their origin at the very heart of the people. To the folk-lorist, the ballad is a spontaneous growth connected originally with the village dance, and common to the primitive rustic life of different races. On the other hand, Courthope found in the ballad the product of a degenerate minstrelsy, working upon a threadbare theme of " romance, lay, or fabliau," or upon some vague historic tradition. Again, Miss Pound largely discounts community and festal origins, and detects traces of ecclesiastical and literary workmanship. All these views seem to contain elements of truth, though the claims of individual authorship need special emphasis. Apart from such questions, the collections of the early and mid-eighteenth century were as important in directing contemporary taste as the miscellanies of Elizabethan days. Ramsay was succeeded by a number of writers, who survive mainly on the reputation of single songs, or as the inventors of themes subsequently handled by Burns. The *Tullochgorum* of John Skinner (1721-1807) in *rime couée* earned the praise of Burns as " the best Scots song Scotland ever saw." Alexander Geddes's (1737-1802) fame rests on *Lewie Gordon*, that of Lady Anne Barnard (1750-1825) upon *Auld Robin Gray*, while Adam Skirving is remembered as the author of *Johnnie Cope*. Everyone knows, too, the *Flowers o' the Forest*, though the name of Jane Elliott, 1727-1805, its composer, has passed into oblivion. It bewails the losses sustained at Flodden Field :

I've heard them lilting at our yowe milking,
Lasses a lilting before the dawn of day:

> But now they are moaning at ilka green loaning—
> The flowers o' the forest are a' wede away.

A pair of writers of greater reputation—the two Hamiltons—form a link between Ramsay and Burns.

Gilbertfield, 1665(?)-1757, as Burns affectionately termed the elder, provided the model for the *Dying Speech of Poor Mailie* in his *Bonny Heck*, and popularized the six-lined stanza used by Fergusson and Burns. The fame of the second Hamilton (of Bangour), 1704-54, rests on the *Braes of Yarrow*, developed round a traditional song and so intimately related to the romantic movement that Wordsworth composed no less than three poems on the same theme—*Yarrow Unvisited, Yarrow Visited, Yarrow Re-visited.*

William Mickle, 1734-88, is remembered by his *Cumnor Hall* which provided the theme of *Kenilworth*, the first stanza, particularly admired by Scott, being probably the best :

> The dews of summer night did fall,
> The moon sweet regent of the sky
> Silvered the walls of Cumnor Hall
> And many an oak that grew thereby.

Two other writers, John Logan, 1748-88, reputed author of the *Cuckoo Song*, and Michael Bruce, 1746-67, known by his verses on *Spring*, bring us to the immediate predecessor of Burns, Robert Fergusson.

It was the fate of Fergusson, the " writer-chiel " (1750-74), to die in a mad-house at the age of twenty-four. Like Collins and Smart, both victims of insanity, Fergusson left a valuable heritage of verse. His *Auld Reikie* and his *Epistles* stand by their own merits, but, otherwise, Fergusson is remembered as the immediate forerunner of Burns. His *Leith Races* supplied the model for the introductory stanzas of the *Holy Fair*, his *Farmer's Ingle* influenced the *Cotter's Saturday Night*, while the *Mutual Complaint of Plainstanes and Causey* is recalled in the *Brigs of Ayr*.

II. THE SECOND PHASE

It remains to mention a certain number of books generally taken as marking the true beginnings of the romantic revival in the south, all of which appeared in, or about, the year 1760. That the beginnings of the movement had shown themselves definitely before this date is clear, but the immediate sensation created by these products of the mid-century was so great that their importance has scarcely been over-estimated. So far, the tendency of romance had lain in the direction of a new interest in natural scenery and in the vernacular dialects—the latter a special feature of northern literature. The immense complexity of later romanticism was scarcely as yet realized. The importance, therefore, of the half-dozen books, belonging roughly to the decade 1760-70, lay in the several directions they pointed out for the future development of romantic aspiration. These are :

Macpherson's *Ossian* (1760-3)
Hurd's *Letters on Chivalry* (1762)
Walpole's *Castle of Otranto* (1764)
Evans's *Specimens of the Poetry of the Ancient Welsh Bards* (1764)
Percy's *Reliques* (1765)
Chatterton's *Rowley Poems* (1768-70)
Warton's *History of English Poetry* (1774-81)

With these the romantic movement in England started in full career, and assumed its characteristic features. The most illuminating suggestions as to the significance of romance have been thrown out by Coleridge, with special application to that aspect which he and Wordsworth illustrated in the *Lyrical Ballads*. The ballad movement and the revived interest in nature, of which signs were apparent early in the century, account for most things in Coleridge and Wordsworth, without the adventitious aid of the new influences that arose in or about the year 1760. Though Wordsworth, Coleridge, and Shelley conceived themselves as imaginatively divining nature, no modern poetry was more creative than this, which steeped itself in the "light which never was on sea or land." It was, accordingly, with a definite attempt to inaugurate a new movement that Coleridge formulated the respective shares that he and Wordsworth were to take in the production of the *Lyrical Ballads*. The personages of Coleridge's verse were to be supernatural, and so handled "as to transfer from our inward nature a human interest and a semblance of truth sufficient to procure for these shadows of imagination that willing suspension of disbelief which constitutes poetic faith." Wordsworth, on the other hand, was to attempt "to give the charm of novelty to things of every day, and to excite a feeling analogous to the supernatural by awakening the mind's attention from the lethargy of custom and directing it to the loveliness and the wonders of the world before us."

With the appearance of Macpherson's *Ossian*, a particular aspect of the ballad movement comes into prominence. Anxiety to publish every available specimen of traditional poetry had sometimes overridden the honesty of compilers, and not a few had tampered with their originals, or inserted contemporary poems and ballads. With Macpherson it was Gaelic literature that drew the attention of the collector, and in his *Fragments of Ancient Poetry Collected in the Highlands* (1760) we possibly have genuine versions of ancient popular epics. With *Fingal* (1762) the case is different, and Macpherson's book is now regarded as a pure concoction. The existence in the north of a body of legends dealing with Finn and Oisin is, of course, well attested, and the outlines of the tradition have been worked out. Oisin, or Ossian, as Macpherson transcribed the name, was the son of Finn mac Cumhaill, whose date is fixed by Irish annalists in the third century A.D. Finn quarrelled with Cormac whose daughter, Grainne, he had married, the feud being handed on to the children, until at the battle of Gabhra Cormac's son, Cairbre, and Finn's grandson, Oscar, fell at each other's hands.

Macpherson's contemporaries varied in their views as to the genuineness of even the *Fragments*, Gray being of opinion that a dull young Scotchman could scarcely have forged his materials. But opposition grew on the appearance of *Fingal* and *Temora*, concerning which Johnson wrote truculently : " Macpherson is so far as I know very quiet. Is not that proof enough ? Everything is against him. No visible manuscript ; no inscription in the language ; no correspondence among friends ; no transaction of business, of which a single scrap remains in the ancient families." But, though somewhat inaccessible to his contemporaries, Macpherson left behind him a number of manuscripts, on which the Highland Society reported, not altogether unfavourably, in 1807. The controversy is still unsettled, though the trend of opinion suggests that Macpherson collected eighteenth century fragments of the cycles, and adapted them to his own ends. His style, despite declamatory and even turgid qualities, is not altogether lacking in the note of regret and vivid feeling for nature, characteristic of the genuine epic. It appealed to its age as " poetry of the heart," and proved a powerful force in directing later movements. In England, Keats has sometimes been claimed as a Celt, and Byron's *Death of Culmar* was a direct imitation of *Ossian*. On the continent, there was a veritable Ossianic furore ; Macpherson's book was done into Italian and Spanish, and created unparalleled enthusiasm in Germany. Herder, Schiller, and Klopstock fell under the spell, and the new poetry displaced Homer in the heart of the sorrowing Werther.

The special note of English romanticism—a revived medievalism, interest in Gothic and the supernatural—

was struck by the appearance of the *Castle of Otranto*, 1764. Though the book was characterized by a contemporary as " such a novel that no boarding-school miss of thirteen could get through it without yawning," it contributed a new element to fiction which was eagerly devoured. Yet the supernaturalism which Walpole handled was neither that of later romanticism, nor that of the great dramatists. It depended for its effect less upon suggestion than upon crude appearances, unrelated to their setting. " Walpole was no poet," said Professor Raleigh, " and the gaiety and inconsequence of his excursions into the supernatural can hardly avoid the suspicion of latent humour. Huge hands and legs clad in armour obtrude themselves at odd moments on the attention of alarmed domestics, whose account of their experiences furnishes the comedy of the book." But this is nineteenth century criticism, and the eighteenth thought otherwise. Writing to Walpole in December, 1764, Gray remarked : " I have received the *Castle of Otranto*, and return you my thanks for it. It engages our attention here (i.e. Cambridge), makes some of us cry a little, and all, in general, afraid to go to bed o' nights. We take it for a translation ; and should believe it to be a true story, were it not for St. Nicholas." Warburton considered it " a masterpiece in the fable," and, before the end of the romantic period, it had earned the praises of both Scott and Byron. The historical importance of the *Castle of Otranto* is considerable—a direct ancestor of the novels of Mrs. Radcliffe, it points through her to the work of that consummate master of romantic fiction, Sir Walter Scott.

The author of this sensational romance was a very different person from what might be imagined. With little poetry in his constitution and a temperament by no means prone to superstition, Walpole moved in aristocratic circles, a fine gentleman and virtuoso. His tastes were social and his love of gossip innate. But his passion for antiquarian pursuits remained unwearied : he was devoted to researches into family history, loved to handle old bric-à-brac, and, at Strawberry Hill, employed himself in adding turrets, towers, and corridors to the nondescript edifice, which had gradually evolved out of Chevenix's cottage.

It was the designer of this Gothic mansion who strove to relieve his ennui by designing a Gothic romance. The genesis of the book is explained in a letter to Cole, the Cambridge antiquary, written in March, 1765. At the outset, Walpole was less communicative, and attempted to shroud his authorship under the guise of anonymity. He must needs practise imposture, and so ally himself with the literary forgers he so heartily despised. (Preface to first edition.)   But, in the second edition, he came forward with an apology and an explanation, which serves to prove his theory in advance of his practice.

The importance of the *Castle of Otranto* is exclusively historical—Walpole lives in literature as a compiler and memoir-writer, and as the most voluminous and gay of correspondents. The weak sides of his character were ferociously laid bare by Macaulay, who pictures him as eccentric, artificial, fastidious, capricious, and the worst of hypocrites : " When the outer disguise of obvious affectation was removed, you were still as far as ever from seeing the real man. He played innumerable parts and over-acted them all." But this is too much. Admitting a certain harshness, a good deal of foppishness, and a proneness to irritability, almost the worst is said. Walpole suffered from irrepressibility of spirits, and his antiquarian researches are illumined by something of the gaiety that has made his memoirs and correspondence so attractive a feature of eighteenth century literature.

The movement inaugurated by Percy's *Reliques* in 1765 ran parallel with the Scottish ballad movement, associated with Ramsay and his successors. Percy's literary activity was almost exclusively confined to the period—some thirty years—during which he was connected with Easton-Maudit, Northamptonshire. At Dromore he had been out of touch with the literary world, and this period, though equally lengthy, proved unproductive. The living of Easton-Maudit, derived from Christ Church, Oxford, gave Percy opportunities for indulging his literary tastes, and, as early as 1761, the firstfruits of his solitude appeared. At the outset, his interest turned to the Far East, both the volume of 1761 and its successor being concerned with Chinese. By 1763, his attention had veered to the north with *Five Pieces of Runic Poetry, translated from the Icelandic,* and to earlier English literature in his edition of Surrey. The *Reliques of Ancient English Poetry,* Percy's title to fame, appeared in 1765, in three volumes. Assistance was freely rendered by Thomas Warton (the younger), Garrick, Grainger, and Goldsmith, and by correspondents in England, Scotland, and Wales. The *Reliques* won an easy popularity and was reprinted from 1767 to 1794. Finally, the translation of Mallet appeared in 1770, Percy's important work being thus produced within the decade 1760-1770.

The *Reliques of Ancient English Poetry* consists of three series, each divided into three books—nine sections in all. Series 1, Book II, is devoted to ballads illustrating Shakespeare, some of which are pure Elizabethan. Though poems were, thus, included which have no claim to be ranked as ballads, this was provided for in the title—" Reliques of Ancient English Poetry, consisting of old heroic ballads, songs and other pieces, of our earlier poets, together with some few of later date." Among these are verses by Hawes, Marlowe, Sir Walter Raleigh, Shakespeare, Warner, Shirley, Daniel, Wotton, Lord Vaux, King James V, Ben Jonson, and even eighteenth century poets like Shenstone, Glover, and Grainger. Percy's object is made clear in the Preface: " To atone for the rudeness of the more obsolete poems, each volume concludes with a few modern attempts in the same kind of writing; and to take off from the tediousness of the longer narratives, they are everywhere intermingled with little elegant pieces of the lyric kind." " Yet," he continues, " perhaps the palm will be frequently due to the old strolling minstrels, who composed their themes to be sung on their harps, and who looked no further than for present applauses and present subsistence "—the worth of which will be realized if contrasted with the following extract from a letter to Dr. Birch (February 2nd, 1765) : " I know not whether you will not be offended to find your name mentioned in the preface of such a strange collection of trash." Probably Percy, like other ballad-collectors, feared ridicule for his venture.

But the book soon won popularity. " I sincerely congratulate you," wrote Dr. Grainger, " on the great success of your ' Ancient Poetry.' The book deserves all the applause which has been given it." Johnson, of course, was not easily reconciled to a type, which he considered well represented by lines like

> I put my hat upon my head
> And walked into the Strand;

and Warburton cynically remarked that " antiquarianism was to true letters what specious funguses are to the oak." The most violent of Percy's critics, however, was Ritson, who opened his attack in the Preface to his *Select Collection of English Songs* (1783), charging him with having forged or garbled his versions.

Percy had stated that the greater part of his material was extracted from an ancient folio manuscript in his possession, containing nearly two hundred poems, songs, and metrical romances. Even this Ritson was not prepared to admit, though he retracted later, making the *amende honorable* in such dubious terms as the following :

The existence and authenticity of this famous manuscript in its present mutilated and miserable condition is no longer to be denied or disputed; at the same time, it is a certain and positive fact, that, in the elegant and refined work it gave occasion to, there is scarcely one single poem, song, or ballad, fairly or honestly printed, either from the above fragment or other alleged authorities, from the beginning to the end. . . . To correct the obvious errors of an illiterate transcriber, to supply irremediable defects, and to make sense of nonsense, are certainly essential duties of an editor of ancient poetry, provided he act with integrity and publicity; but secretly to suppress the original text, and insert his own fabrications for the sake of providing more refined entertainment for readers of taste and genius is no proof of either judgment, candour or integrity.

Was Ritson right? The answer may be found in the Hales and Furnivall edition of the actual folio manuscript, which Percy declared he found " lying dirty on the floor in a bureau in the parlour " of his friend, Humphrey Pitt, of Shifnall, Shropshire, " being used by the maids to light the fire." In the first place, only 45 out of 176 pieces in the *Reliques* are borrowed from the folio, though this contained 191 songs and ballads. Secondly, he doctored his text. In Furnivall's words : " He puffed out the 39 lines of the *Child of Eld* to 200 ; he pomatumed the *Heir of Linne* till it shone again ; he stuffed bits of wool into *Sir Cawline* and *Sir Aldingar*; he powdered everything." Yet, in the end, our debt to Percy remains enormous. He was the first to print *Sir Patrick Spens*, *Sir Cawline*, and *King Estmere* among other things, though sufficiently careless to allow the original of the last to be lost at the printer's. Wordsworth was not slow to recognize his achievement and contrasted Percy with both Macpherson and Bürger to the Englishman's advantage, summing up as follows : " I have already stated how much Germany is indebted to this latter work ; and for our own country, its poetry has been absolutely redeemed by it. I do not think that there is an able writer in verse of the present day who would not be proud to acknowledge his obligations to the ' Reliques '; I know that it is so with my friends ; and, for myself, I am happy in this occasion to make a public avowal of my own " (Essay supplementary to the Preface of 1815).

The importance of the *Rowley Poems* (1768-70) lies in the fact that they stimulated interest in early English literature. Tyrwhitt's *Chaucer* (1775) marked an epoch in the study of medieval literature, but was anticipated by a series of poems, which could not fail to arouse general interest in the fifteenth century. Possessed of an almost consuming passion for obsolete diction and spelling, Chatterton's interest in old books remained unbounded from the day when the illuminated capitals of an old French music-folio first caught his eye. The office of sexton at the parish church of St. Mary Redcliffe had been held as an hereditary office by his paternal ancestors for nearly two centuries, and, at this particular moment, was occupied by his uncle. Chatterton devoted his out-of-school hours to heraldic designs, sketches of old armour and architecture. The manuscript contents of the chest in the muniment-room at St. Mary Redcliffe's were rapidly dispersed, fragments finding their way into the boy's hands. Having already produced some original verse, Chatterton was now to apply his skill to questionable purposes.

In 1764—if we may trust the story—he sent the junior usher of the Blue Coat school a discoloured piece of parchment, containing *Elinoure and Juga,* and succeeded in convincing him of its genuineness. He had been reading Speght's *Chaucer* and compiling a glossary of obsolete words, based on the dictionaries of Kersey and Bailey, and, from this, material found its way into the poem—e.g., *inhild,* to infuse, *limed,* polished, *linche,* bank, and, with modification of meaning, *lyped,* wasted away, *miskynette,* bagpipe, etc. The imposture succeeded, and he was emboldened in 1767 to speak of the discovery of the De Bergham arms, together with a pedigree showing the family's descent from one of the Conqueror's knights.

During the same year, Chatterton was engaged on a series of poems, which he afterwards put forward as the work of Thomas Rowley, a secular priest of the fifteenth century and friend of William Canynge, mayor of Bristol, though the name was probably derived from an epitaph in St. John's Church, Bristol, recounting the death in 1478 of one Thomas Rowley, merchant.

In 1768, in connexion with the opening of a bridge at Bristol, Chatterton wrote to the editor of *Felix Farley's Bristol Journal*, enclosing a prose description " from an old manuscript " of the mayor's first crossing of the ancient bridge in 1248, but the authorship he afterwards admitted to a friend, John Rudhall. Towards the close of the year, he sent to George Catcott a succession of Rowley poems—the *Bristowe Tragedie* (printed 1772), the *Epitaph on Robert Canynge*, a *Challenge to Lydgate*, and the *Song to Ælla*, though he is said to have privately admitted his authorship of the first piece.

Chatterton wrote to Walpole in 1769, enclosing a prose treatise, *The Ryse of Peyncteynge yn Englande, wroten by T. Rowleie,* 1469, *for Mastre Canynge.* Enthusiastic at the outset, Walpole showed the material to Gray, who pronounced it a forgery, and the return of the manuscript was long delayed. No doubt, Chatterton failed to understand how the author of the *Castle of Otranto* could be offended by this mild deception.

On April 14th, 1770, Chatterton wrote a *Last Will and Testament*, "composed between eleven and two o'clock on Saturday, in the utmost distress of mind." He started for London in April, and there subscribed to the magazines, but without adequate remuneration. July saw the completion of the *Excelent Balade of Charity* which was refused by the *Town and County Magazine*, and with the *Revenge* he was little more successful. In August, he talked of going abroad as a surgeon, but before the end of the month was dead, poisoned by his own hand.

The critical camp was for long divided over the literary merits of Chatterton's work, but the final word as to its linguistic value was pronounced by Skeat, who showed that neither in verse-form, language, nor rhymes could the poems claim to be older than the eighteenth century. Chatterton's method seems to have been to copy archaic words from the dictionaries of Kersey and Bailey into a glossary, upon which he subsequently based his fictions. If, then, it was with "sham antiques" that he hoaxed his contemporaries, what is their value for posterity? The intrinsic worth of the *Rowley Poems* consists in their underlying vein of romance and in their realization of the undreamt beauties of ancient diction. Chatterton understood the suggestive power latent in names, and embodied his narrative in a setting, which the ear of the antiquarian may easily miss. His precocity was amazing, considering that these poems, ascribed to the reign of Edward IV, were the work of a youth who died at eighteen. All is not equal, but there is, at least, the *Excelent Balade of Charity* with its anticipations of Keats's *Eve of St. Agnes*, the *Unknown Knight* foreshadowing the *Christabel* metre, and *Ælla* with its exquisite *Minstrel's Song* :

> O sing unto my roundelay,
> O drop the briny tear with me,
> Dance no more at holy-day,
> Like a running river be.
> My love is dead,
> Gone to his death-bed,
> All under the willow-tree.

> Black his locks as the winter night,
> White his skin as the summer snow,
> Red his face as the morning light,
> Cold he lies in the grave below.
> My love is dead,
> Gone to his death-bed,
> All under the willow-tree.

The intense interest aroused by Chatterton's work and the growing suspicion as to its genuineness is illustrated by a passage on Rowley in Thomas Warton's *History of English Poetry* (1774-81)—a book, which itself holds an important place in the series of literary ventures, inaugurating the romantic revival. Warton devoted several pages to Rowley, but concludes significantly : " It must be acknowledged that there are some circumstances which incline us to suspect these pieces to be a modern forgery." The *History* itself was the first serious attempt to produce a chronological record of the progress of English literature from the thirteenth century onwards, with abundant quotation and critical dicta. The task had been unessayed before Warton, though Gray and Pope had each planned a history. An important series of *Observations on Spenser* (1754) gives Warton further claim to be regarded as a pioneer romantic, representing, as it does, an attempt to reinstate the *Faerie Queene*. Unfortunately, Warton undervalued Spenser's stanza. Further, there are his important Miltonic sonnets, including that " written in a blank leaf of Dugdale's *Monasticon* " :

> Deem not devoid of elegance the sage,
> By Fancy's genuine feelings unbeguiled,
> Of painful pedantry the poring child,
> Who turns, of these proud domes, th' historic page,
> Now sunk by Time, and Henry's fiercer rage.
> Think'st thou the warbling Muses never smiled
> On his lone hours? Ingenuous views engage
> His thoughts, on themes, unclassic falsely styled,
> Intent. While cloistered Piety displays
> Her mouldering roll, the piercing eye explores
> New manners, and the pomp of elder days,
> Whence culls the pensive bard his pictured stores.
> Nor rough nor barren are the winding ways
> Of hoar Antiquity, but strown with flowers.

In appreciation of Spenser Warton must yield the palm to Bishop Hurd, whose *Letters on Chivalry* appeared in 1762. It is historical, as opposed to philosophic, investigation, which alone, in Hurd's view, can set us at the right point of view with regard to the Middle Ages, for chivalry and its concomitants were an outcome of feudalism, and of that alone. Medieval romance he regarded as the work of inferior poets, though, at its best, it compares favourably with the epics of ancient Greece, which it even surpasses in dignity, magnificence, and variety. But all is " enchanted ground." It is a fault in moderns to judge romance by recent canons. " Gothic " has its own rules, by which, when it comes to be tested, it is seen to possess merits as great as the " Grecian." Accordingly, we must not apply the laws of one period to another more remote, for poetry has its own laws, and the poet moves in a world of his own fancy. The cry : " Follow Nature " is, therefore, a fallacy.

" What we have gotten by this revolution, you will say, is a great deal of good sense. What we have lost is a world of fine fabling ; the illusion of which is so grateful to the charmed spirit ; that, in spite of philosophy and fashion, Faery Spenser still ranks highest among the poets ; I mean with all those who are either come of that house or have any kindness for it. Earth-born critics, my friend, may blaspheme,

> But all the Gods are ravished with delight
> Of his celestial song, and music's wondrous might."

Brief mention may be made, lastly, of another book, *Some Specimens of the Poetry of the Ancient Welsh Bards*, by the Rev. Evan Evans (1764). This inspired Gray's *Triumphs of Owen* (1768), and, along with *Ossian*, assisted in promoting that special aspect of the romantic revival known as the Celtic movement.

With these works romanticism started in full career and in a score of directions. The complexity of the movement, when it came full tide, cannot be better illustrated than by the dictum we owe to Brunetière : " Romanticism means liberty in art, substitution of individual impulse for the sense of the community, a heightening of the sentiment of self, a passage from the objective to the subjective, from oratory and drama to elegy, cosmopolitanism, an interest in the past, the introduction of the methods and aims of painting, and a new feeling for nature."

VIII

THE EARLY ROMANTICS

I. COWPER

BETWEEN the death of Gray in 1771 and the appearance of the *Lyrical Ballads* (1798) the most conspicuous among English poets were Cowper, Burns, and Blake, and particular significance is accordingly associated with the dates of their chief productions—Blake's *Poetical Sketches* (1783), Cowper's *Task* (1785), and the Kilmarnock edition of Burns's poems (1786). All were pioneers of the romantic movement, but each in his own way.

Contrasted with Pope, Cowper is the typical English domestic poet. Experience had dealt hardly with him in his early years, and he shrank from the stir and bustle of affairs to seek shelter, where none but sympathetic eyes might meet his. In the *Tirocinium or Review of Schools* (1785), he pleaded earnestly for private as against public tuition on the score of the brutality practised in public institutions. Cowper seems to have had reason on his side, if we credit his statement that he knew his bullying schoolfellow " better by his shoe-buckles than by any other part of his dress." On the period of his apprenticeship to the law he was wont to look back with regret. *Dilecto volo lascivire sodali* is, however, a motto natural to youth, and, in Cowper's case, contact with mundane affairs was scarcely too protracted for the tasks at hand. If we recall the shadow so near at hand, no regret need be felt that the poet had condescended for a moment to be glad and gay.

Cowper had applied for the office of Clerk of the

Journals of the House of Lords, and ran the risk of securing the appointment. To one of his temperament the prospect was alarming, in that it entailed a preliminary examination at the bar of the House. " A thunderbolt would have been as welcome to me as this intelligence. I knew, to demonstration, that upon these terms the clerkship of the journals was no place for me. . . . They whose spirits are formed like mine, to whom a public exhibition of themselves, on any occasion, is mortal poison, may have some idea of the horrors of my situation; others can have none." At length, as the crisis approached, he meditated suicide, afterwards declining rapidly into religious mania.

In 1765 Cowper moved to Huntingdon, where it was his good fortune to meet the Unwins. In a letter to his cousin, Mrs. Cowper (October 20th, 1766), he gives an account of the daily routine in the Unwin family, embodied in a perfect picture of domestic felicity. Always sensitive to religious impressions, he began at Olney to compose hymns, many of which have become a permanent possession among Englishmen. Not too often has religious poetry been written with success. It tends to a monotony of splendour, and is apt to lose itself in abstractions; it serves to confirm faith, but itself needs to be buttressed thereby. Yet Cowper stands, by his contributions to English hymnology, in the first rank of religious poets.

During the winter of 1780-1, he began his career as an author with the *Progress of Error, Truth, Table Talk*, and *Expostulation*, published with additions under the title *Poems by William Cowper, of the Inner Temple, Esq.* (1782). Here, Cowper reveals himself as a follower of Pope; the metre is the heroic couplet and the themes abstract. But, in common with other revolters, Cowper permitted himself licence, particularly in the manipulation of the cæsura and the lengthening of the line. There is even a direct attack on the Popeian method itself :

> When labour and when dullness, club in hand,
> Like the two figures at St. Dunstan's stand,
> Beating alternately, in measur'd time,
> The clock-work tintinabulum of rhyme,
> Exact and regular the sounds will be,
> But such mere quarter-strokes are not for me,
> > —*Table Talk*

and Pope, in well-known lines, is charged with having reduced poetry to mere artifice :

> But he (his musical finesse was such,
> So nice his ear, so delicate his touch)
> Made poetry a mere mechanic art,
> And every warbler has his tune by heart.
> > —*Table Talk*.

The main excellence of this group consists in the sketches, embedded in the framework of the argument —those of the sportsman, " the Nimrod of the neighbouring lairs " (*Progress of Error*), the cleric,

> Himself a wanderer from the narrow way,
> His silly sheep, what wonder if they stray?
> > —*Progress of Error*

the hermit,

> Wearing out life in his religious whim,
> Till his religious whimsy wears out him,
> > —*Truth*

the ancient prude, one of the masterpieces of the collection, and, finally, Voltaire.

The note of patriotism, characteristic of the later *Task,* is anticipated in *Table Talk* in the eloquent lines to freedom, which associate Cowper with the pioneers of the reform movement. The closest approach to Pope's art is to be found in the lines on card-playing in the *Progress of Error* with their added note of satire, for which the *Rape of the Lock* offered no suggestion.

The volume of 1782 was, however, eclipsed by the *Task* (1785), which, like *John Gilpin,* owed its suggestion to Cowper's new-found friend, Lady Austen. The medium—blank verse—permitted of discursive description, and, though Cowper had as yet hardly attained to the mastery of *Yardley Oak* (1797), his command

of the new metre was already considerable. Putting
aside such things as the anapæstic *Selkirk* (1781),
the *Royal George* (1782), the lines on the *Receipt
of his Mother's Picture* (1790), *To Mary* (1793), and
the *Castaway* (1799), the *Task* may be said to supply
those characteristics of Cowper's work which mark him
most clearly a pioneer of romanticism. In the first
place, if Pope proved himself the poet of eighteenth
century civic life, Cowper was no less distinctly its
domestic poet. Despite his enthusiasm for the country
and country walks, the centre of comfort to Cowper was
always the domestic hearth. He is, as Sainte-Beuve
declared, *le poète du chez soi*, and his favourite theme
the delights of a winter evening.

> Ante larem proprium placidam expectare senectam,
> Tum demum exactis non infeliciter annis,
> Sortiri tacitum lapidem, aut sub cespite condi.
>
> —*Votum.*

Often must he have reciprocated the sentiment of
Horace's line—*O noctes cœnæque deum*—to which he
himself gives poetic expresssion in the fourth book of
the *Task*. To bohemian tastes there is something
offensive in this quiet domesticity with its prominent
tea-urn, and Byron could think of Cowper merely as the
" coddled poet." Yet he amply fulfils his function as
the poet of typical English country-life; his large
enthusiasm for sights and sounds continues the Thom-
sonian tradition and marks a break with Pope. He is
capable both of minute description and of a perspective,
whereby objects in the foreground tend to stand out
distinct, and he describes from long familiarity :

> Scenes must be beautiful which daily viewed
> Please daily, and whose novelty survives
> Long knowledge and the scrutiny of years.

The *Task* contains, further, a number of sketches
remarkable for both accuracy and detail—sketches of
the woodman accompanied by his dog,

> Shaggy and lean, and shrewd, with pointed ears
> And tail cropp'd short, half lurcher and half cur,

and of the gipsies, skilful

> To conjure clean away the gold they touch,
> Conveying worthless dross into its place.

Though the effect of realistic description does not depend entirely upon choice of subject, Cowper chose to handle the more pleasant themes. That he had some affinity with Crabbe is apparent from the account of the morning walk and the underlying tone of irony in the description of indoor games in Book IV :

> Time, as he passes us, has a dove's wing,
> Unsoil'd and swift, and of a silken sound;
> But the world's time is time in masquerade.
> Theirs, should I paint him, has his pinions fledg'd
> With motley plumes, and where the peacock shows
> His azure eyes, is tinctured black and red
> With spots quadrangular of di'mond form,
> Ensanguin'd hearts, clubs typical of strife,
> And spades, the emblem of untimely graves.

But a distinctly Christian note pervades both his general argument and his appreciation of nature. The famous line,

> God made the country, and man made the town

suggests one of the directions along which Cowper came to regard nature as man's counsellor. From another aspect, there is in the *Task*, Book III, a passage of moving eloquence, indicating that for a time he had freed himself from the religious despair, to which he surrendered in the agonizing lines of the *Castaway* :

> I was a stricken deer that left the herd
> Long since; with many an arrow deep infixt,
> My panting side was charg'd, when I withdrew
> To seek a tranquil death in distant shades.
> There was I found by one who had himself
> Been hurt by th' archers. In his side he bore,
> And in his hands and feet, the cruel scars.
> With gentle force soliciting the darts,
> He drew them forth, and healed and bade me live.

In his somewhat rambling method, Cowper is, again, akin to Crabbe, yet just as he shrank from contact with

living bohemians, so he avoided anything approaching
literary scurrility. It has 'been objected that nature
served him merely as a background, of which he failed
to penetrate the secrets. No doubt, his affinities were
closer with Rousseau than with Wordsworth—the day
of Wordsworthian mysticism was as yet far off—but a
philosophy of nature was not wanting, and is expounded
in a number of passages. It is Cowper who speaks in
the fifth book of the *Task* of

> The unambiguous footsteps of the God
> Who gives its lustre to an insect's wing
> And wheels his throne upon the rolling worlds,

who, in Book VI, asserts

> The Lord of all, himself through all diffused,
> Sustains and is the life of all that lives,

supporting his doctrine by the eloquent lines :

> Not a flower
> But shows some touch in freikle, streak, or stain,
> Of his unrivall'd pencil.

From the eighteenth century point of view, Cowper
was a poet of revolt, yet he provides occasional examples
of poetic diction in keeping with the pseudo-classic style.
His Latinisms sometimes remind us of the worst offences
of Thomson and Armstrong, though allowance must be
made for his love of burlesque, illustrated frequently in
the *Letters*. These represent him in his most charming
pose as the lover of domestic delights, apt to raillery
when the mood seizes him, fond of chattering about
books, hares, gardening, or landscape—in fact, capable
of entertaining his correspondents most highly when he
professes to have nothing to say. Instance the following
letter :

THE LODGE,
December 10th, 1787.

To Lady Hesketh

I thank you for the snip of cloth, commonly called
a pattern. At present I have two coats, and but one

back. If at any time hereafter I should find myself possessed of fewer coats, or more backs, it will be of use to me.

Even as you suspect, my dear, so it proved. The ball was prepared for, the ball was held, and the ball passed, and we had nothing to do with it. Mrs. Throckmorton, knowing our trim, did not give us the pain of an invitation, for a pain it would have been. And why? as Sternhold says—Because, as Hopkins answers, we must have refused it. But it fell out singularly enough that this ball was held, of all the days in the year, on my birthday—and so I told them—but not till it was all over.

Though I have thought proper never to take notice of the arrival of my manuscripts together with the *other good things* in the box, yet certain it is, that I received them. I have furbished up the tenth book till it is as bright as silver, and am now occupied in bestowing the same labour upon the eleventh. The twelfth and thirteenth are in the hands of ——, and the fourteenth and fifteenth are ready to succeed them. This notable job is the delight of my heart, and how sorry shall I be when it is ended.

The smith and the carpenter, my dear, are both in the room, hanging a bell; if I therefore make a thousand blunders, let the said intruders answer for them all.

I thank you, my dear, for your history of the G——s. What changes in the family! And how many thousand families have in the same time experienced changes as violent as theirs! The course of a rapid river is the justest of all emblems, to express the variableness of our scene below. Shakespeare says none ever bathed himself twice in the same stream, and it is equally true that the world upon which we close our eyes at night is never the same with that on which we open them in the morning.

I do not always say, give my love to my uncle, because he knows that I always love him. I do not always present Mrs. Unwin's love to you, partly for the same reason—Deuce take the smith and the carpenter !—and partly because I forget it. But to present my own I forget never, for I always have to finish my letter, which I know not how to do, my dearest Coz, without telling you that I am ever yours,

W.C.

II. BURNS

When Burns wrote out the substance of his own epitaph, he meant it to point a moral rather than to adorn a tale :

> The poor inhabitant below
> Was quick to learn and wise to know
> And keenly felt the friendly glow
>   And softer flame,
> But thoughtless follies laid him low
>   And stained his name.

The world, however, has not cared to finally judge Burns; it has often preferred to take him for its teacher. A poet whose sympathy reaches out to the everyday life of the people wins a place in the national heart unconsciously. Just in so far as the ideas at the back of his verse are common to himself and the nation, to that extent is his poetry recognized as real. The poet becomes the national representative, and bears on his work the impress not only of his own individuality, but of the race from which he is sprung.

It is by mere fortune of time that the name of Burns has been handed down. Born in an earlier age, he might have remained a nameless balladist—at one with the authors of *Sir Patrick Spens*, of *Burd Helen*, and *Edom O'Gordon*. It was a sinister fate that denied the poet anonymity and made of him a type. The world would have remained satisfied with his verse, and have been spared discussion of his character.

Just here, in their closeness to national life, is it that

poets like Burns and Béranger are to be distinguished from the peculiarly literary class. Burns was not the first, but the last great poet of Scotland. A land, which had resounded with song from the days of Bruce, brought him forth that he might catch the living utterances from the lips of the people, and give them imperishable form. The mystery of Burns is none other than the eternal mystery—the mystery of genius. All his material lay to hand, even that of his best known work. The *Cotter's Saturday Night*, the *Brigs of Ayr*, the *Holy Fair*, *John Barleycorn*—none of these things are original. The saying of Molière, " *Je prends mon bien où je le trouve*," is applicable to Burns no less than to Shakespeare and the older dramatists. But the charming *naïveté*, with which the Scottish poet borrows whole stanzas from his predecessors, is less easy to parallel.

To consider Burns a mere "snapper-up of unconsidered trifles" would, however, be unjust. It is true that the refrains and choruses of many of his songs —*John Anderson My Jo*, *Auld Lang Syne*, *Duncan Gray*, *Ay Waukin' O*, *O'er the Water to Charlie*—are unoriginal, that a piece like *It was a' for our Rightfu' King* is a re-writing of *Mally Stewart*, and *A Red, Red Rose* a pastiche from a multiplicity of sources. For Burns's method was to ransack the song-books, to adopt a title or a hint, to rearrange, omit, condense. But the refrain from the *Tea-Table Miscellany*,

> For the sake o' Somebody,
> For the sake o' Somebody,
> I could wake a winter night
> For the sake o' Somebody,

is subjected to the subtlest of variations, and becomes in his hands a thing of beauty. That Burns held serious views of his art is apparent from his numerous revisions, his suppressed stanzas, and the successive versions of poems like *Ca' the Yowes to the Knowes* and *Ye Banks and Braes*. His triumph was to have rescued such things for the world by imparting to them his sovereign impress.

There have been those, who have declaimed against Burns because of a distate for the world, in which he moved—that world, as Matthew Arnold put it, of Scotch drink, Scotch religion, and Scotch manners. It lies in the nature of things that the work of any writer must possess limitations—those of his personality, of his language, of the age in which he is born. But Burns's work is most characteristic where he limits himself most in time and space—in the *Jolly Beggars, Hallowe'en,* the *Address to the Deil,* and *Poor Mailie,* in the satires, epistles, and epitaphs. What was left for the artist to perform Burns has accomplished with a sovereign touch, which imparts to his creations the moving energy of life.

To inquire how far questions of individuality enter into art is not altogether profitable. If Marlowe was an atheist he had, at least, a magnificent soaring intellect which transports; if Swift, feeling himself decaying from the top, embraced mankind in one ramifying hatred, he had, at least, a gift of satire which he has bestowed freely on the race; if Blake was mad rather than sane, he had a command of pathos which touches almost to tears. And Burns, typical though he be of the natural man in his frailty, has yet a power over the human heart which renders him an eternal possession.

It is a far cry from Dumfries to Edinburgh. Little wonder, then, that, when the glamour of a wider literary fame fell upon the poet, he should have masqueraded in a new-fashioned dress. Henceforth, the woes of Sylvander and his passion for Clarinda formed the subject of his verse :

> Clarinda, mistress of my soul,
> The measured time is run !
> The wretch beneath the dreary pole
> So marks his latest sun.

> To what dark cave of frozen night
> Shall poor Sylvander hie?
> Deprived of thee, his life and light,
> The sun of all his joy.

To such bathos can a poet descend, when he deserts his natural vernacular in the endeavour after a more literary diction. Even in his best English verse, where the poet has turned moralist and supplied a fruitful source of quotation to latter-day preachers—in the *Cotter's Saturday Night*, in *A Man's a Man*, in *An Epistle to a Young Friend*—we miss the natural Burns.

Burns has become a perennial subject, but the secret of his charm is not far to seek. It is in his sense of *passion* that he is at one with the greatest poets. Earth, sea, and sky are to him but a symbol of his own heart. He dwells in an enchanted land

> Where the daisies are rose-scented,
> And the rose itself has got
> Perfume which on earth is not.

If for other kinds of perfection we turn elsewhere—to Heine, to Shelley, to the songs of Greece, to the ballads and lyrics of old France—it is to Burns that we look for impassioned expression in its simplest and most natural form—to the *Cauld Blast*, *Of a' the Airts*, and *My Nanie, O*.

III. BLAKE

An investigator into the history of the early romantic movement finds himself confronted with many problems, but few more difficult of solution than those associated with Blake. His aloofness from the general trend of poetic thought in his day, his complete emancipation from convention, his extraordinary sensitiveness to unseen influences, his idiosyncrasies—all these particularities mark him out a unique figure in the literary movement of the century. It may well be doubted whether any country or age has produced a literary phenomenon exactly comparable to this eighteenth century mystic.

Since Cowper laid it down that " God made the country, and man made the town," it has been usual to associate the romantic spirit with wide tracts and mountains. But it was London, the queen of cities, that gave birth to Blake, and, in the vicinity of London, he met his choirs of angels. As a boy, Blake saw visions and dreamed dreams. He was but four years old when, according to a story recounted by his wife, " God put his forehead to the window and set him a-screaming." Throughout his life he remained a visionary.

Blake's father was a Swedenborgian, and the son's productions show traces of the father's faith. But Blake was no more an orthodox Swedenborgian than an orthodox romantic : his faith remained his own and he acknowledged no master :

> I must create a system, or be enslaved by another Man's,
> I will not Reason and Compare: my business is to create.
> —*Jerusalem.*

Blake received no schooling, but took lessons in drawing and became apprenticed to an engraver. At the age of twenty, he set up for himself as engraver to the booksellers, and contributed to Harrison's *Novelists' Magazine* a series of eight engravings, based on designs by Stothard. In 1784 he opened a printseller's shop in Broad Street, and ten years later established himself in Hercules Buildings, Lambeth, as illustrator of Young's *Night Thoughts.* In 1800 he took up residence with Hayley, Cowper's biographer, his function being to illustrate the new volume. Three years later, he returned to London, where he remained for the rest of his life, neglected by the outside public, but lovingly cherished by a small circle of friends, until he passed away serenely in August, 1827. " I cannot think of death," he once remarked, " as more than the going out of one room into another."

The appearance of Blake's *Poetical Sketches* in 1783

was in the nature of a literary phenomenon. Neither Cowper's *Task* nor Burns's Kilmarnock poems had yet been published, and the day of Wordsworth and Coleridge was as yet far off. The tone of the period is best represented by Hayley's *Triumphs of Temper* (1781) and Erasmus Darwin's *Botanic Garden* (1789-92). The revolters, indeed, included Crabbe, whose *Village* had appeared in the same year as the *Poetical Sketches*, but so long as Johnson survived it seemed unlikely that anything in the nature of a serious break would be countenanced. The publication of Blake's volume was assisted by Flaxman and other members of his *côterie*. As for the public, they turned a cold shoulder on the venture which fell stillborn from the press. It is true that the real Blake was not fully revealed in this early volume, but there was surely enough for wonderment. The poems on the seasons—spring, summer, autumn, and winter—betray a trace of Spenser, but the rich toning recalls Keats and a later manner :

> O Autumn, laden with fruit, and stained
> With the blood of the grape, pass not, but sit
> Beneath my shady roof; there thou mayst rest,
> And tune thy jolly voice to my fresh pipe,
> And all the daughters of the year shall dance!
> Sing now thy lusty song of fruits and flowers.

There is a suggestion of Collins in the personifications of *To the Evening Star* and *To Morning*, but, for the chiselled verse of the English classicist, Blake substitutes a glow and throb, anticipatory of a newer method. In the same way, the ballads of *Fair Elenor* and *Gwin, King of Norway*, are utterly different from the *rifacimenti* beloved of eighteenth century practitioners. The style is often tumid and the metre faltering, but the tumidity is never far removed from magnificence :

> The god of war is drunk with blood;
> The earth doth faint and fail;
> The stench of blood makes sick the heavens,
> Ghosts glut the throat of hell,
>
> —*Gwin*

while *Elenor* culminates in a passage of imaginative sensibility, unsurpassed even in the genuine ballads.

Blake's patriotism finds expression in a poem, for which the war-songs of England offer no parallel in respect of chastened moral vision, and, as final examples, there are the *Mad Song*—a triumph of technical skill— and the address *To the Muses*, with its bitter note of regret for things gone by. But the mere suggestion of imitation, combined with the absence of certain notes, which appreciation has come to associate with the name of Blake, sets the *Poetical Sketches*, as a whole, on a lower level than the later volumes—the *Songs of Innocence* (1789) and the *Songs of Experience* (1794).

The *Songs of Innocence* was produced—binding, papers, and contents—by the unaided efforts of Blake and his wife, according to a new process revealed to him in a dream. It constitutes one of the rarities of literary bibliography. The *Songs of Innocence* represent Blake's philosophy of childhood—if such can be called philosophy, into which the meddling intellect is never permitted to intrude. For Blake admits no truce with reason, and it is the combination of simplicity with an undertone of mysticism that makes this volume of child verses unique. From a heart, which retained throughout life the emotions characteristic of the child, Blake gave expression to childish wonder and joy, as in the *Songs of Experience* he was to give expression to childish dread. All animated creation, viewed from the child standpoint, unites in the pæan of joy, childish laughter being echoed from the hills by the " lamb's innocent call " and the chirp of the " painted birds." *Infant Joy*, the title of one of the poems, thus becomes the sub-title of the whole volume. But experience gave Blake his glimpses of sorrow, and the tone of the *Songs of Experience* is saddened. Fortunately, he was able to reconcile the two visions, and the sum of his teaching on this matter is embodied in three lines:

> Man was made for joy and woe;
> And when this we rightly know,
> Safely through the world we go.

The anticipations in Blake of the directions, which poetry was to take later, are not easily reckoned. If Wordsworth turned his attention to the life diffused throughout all created things, Blake was drawn towards field and flower and bird, as to creatures fully sentient, and summoned all to join in the communion of bliss :

> Arise, you little glancing wings, and sing your infant joy,
> Arise and drink your bliss!
> For everything that lives is holy.

At those who would work harm he points a warning finger :

> He who torments the chafer's sprite,
> Weaves a bower in endless night.
> The caterpillar on the leaf
> Repeats to thee thy mother's grief.
> Kill not the moth nor butterfly
> For the last judgment draweth nigh.

This is a more highly spiritualized philosophy than even Wordsworth's, and Blake was a revolutionary before Cowper or Burns. He counted Paine among his personal friends, and was himself regarded as a Jacobin. He had no respect for caste or privilege, counting priest-craft as nought, but duty leavens his patriotism and love his spiritual philosophy. Blake was a naturalist before Cowper and a mystic before Coleridge, but his mysticism carried him farther than the romantics, and there is no parallel in the later school for the absolved view of created universe, to which he gave expression in both prose and verse :

> Heaven opens here on all sides her golden gates; her windows are not obstructed by vapours; voices of the celestial inhabitants are more distinctly heard and their forms more distinctly seen; and my cottage is also a shadow of their houses.

IX

POLITICAL WRITERS AND PERIODICAL REVIEWERS

THE outbreak of the French Revolution, in the stupendous events of 1789, has been traced to many causes—the absolutism of the Bourbon monarchy, voiced by Louis XIV in the magnificent dictum, *L'état c'est moi*, the frivolity and weakness of his successor, the monopoly and privileges enjoyed by the feudal orders, and the wretched condition of the proletariat during the second half of the century, the results of which were foreshadowed in Madame de Pompadour's dictum : "After us the deluge." The intellectual revolt of the century must also be reckoned with, and, though Carlyle was right in his condemnation of "victorious analysis" and the "endless vortices of froth-logic," it is here that the link between English and French political thought is most apparent.

Lord Acton assigned to Fénelon a pioneer position among French revolutionary thinkers, as "the first man who saw through the majestic hypocrisy of the Court and knew that France was on the road to ruin." In quick succession followed Montesquieu, Voltaire, Rousseau, Diderot, and D'Alembert—all of whom ultimately derived their scepticism and ideas of freedom from English writers, like Newton, Locke, Shaftesbury, and Bolingbroke. But revolutionary ideals gained a new colour and lease of life abroad, and the French became, in their turn, the inspirers of the English. The propagandas of Jean Jacques Rousseau, centring in the doctrine that "Man was born free and is everywhere in chains," were, by reason of their emotional colouring, the most far-reaching. His *Social Contract* affected the phraseology of the American Declaration of Rights, while his gospel of humanity was accepted by enthusiasts as a matter of faith. But, in England, Rousseau lost credit as time went on, and the old enthusiasm gradually disappeared, though ideas ultimately inspired by him are apparent everywhere in the political theory, no less than the poetry, of the revolutionary epoch.

Among the various shades of political opinion existing in England during the revolutionary epoch Burke stands out as the representative of the Old Whig or Conservative party. His position was first made apparent with all the force of his intellect in the *Thoughts on the Cause of the Present Discontents* (1770), where the case for the people is maintained against that of the King's party, so-called. Though unwilling to consider the people always in the right, Burke declares " that in all disputes between them and their rulers, the presumption is at least upon a par in favour of the people." This is a cautious judgment, but some of the observations suggest the breadth of view of Burke's later declarations, especially those relating to the party system. " Our constitution," he declared, " stands on a nice equipoise, with steep precipices and deep waters upon all sides of it. In removing it from a dangerous leaning towards one side, there may be a risk of oversetting it on the other." With this in mind, Burke goes on to oppose an extension of the suffrage, more frequent parliaments, the disenfranchisement of rotten boroughs, and similar proposals. He was assuredly no democrat, and, from the point of view of practical politics, was probably right in opposing such ideals at this juncture.

The three famous declarations on American policy— the *Speech on American Taxation* (April, 1774), that on *Conciliation* (1775), and the *Letter to the Sheriffs of Bristol* (1777)—reveal Burke on his noblest and most philosophical side. They compose an eloquent and reasoned plea for justice and freedom, actuated by a lofty moral outlook. " What," he asked, " is war but a fallacy, what national pride but a sophism ? " To the argument that English action was dictated by sovereign right his reply was : " I am not here going into the distinctions of rights, nor attempting to mark their boundaries. I do not enter into these metaphysical distinctions. I hate the very sound of them." And, in a magnificent summary of the whole argument : " I do not know the method of drawing up an indictment against a whole people."

The attitude which Burke maintained in the *Reflections* has been regarded differently by different thinkers, but it would be hard to discover anyone, who was prepared either to support or denounce Burke at all points. The *Reflections* was a piece of work deliberately planned, representing the labour of a full year. The principles, upon which it was based, were the tried convictions of one, who may be claimed as the first of our political philosophers. The Revolution is attacked, precisely because it was revolutionary. There could, in Burke's view, be no violent severance with the past without the direst consequences. International relations would inevitably suffer, and, just as a man is influenced by his neighbourhood, so nation by nation. In words prophetic of the position he was to occupy later, Burke declares : " France has always more or less influenced manners in England; and when your fountain is choked up and polluted, the stream will not run along, or run clear, with us, or perhaps any nation." With the greatest contempt, Burke looked around upon the gerrymandering schemes, proposed by members of the Constitutional Club, and the doctrine of abstract rights which was everywhere enunciated. His judgment was determined by practical considerations. " What is the use of discussing a man's abstract right to food or to medicine ? The question is upon the method of procuring and administering them." Yet he has his own

conception of these : " The rights of men in govern-
ments are their advantages; and these are often in
balances between differences of good; in compromises
sometimes between good and evil, and sometimes
between evil and evil. Political reason is a computing
principle." And again : " Believe me, sir, those who
attempt to level never equalize."

But, despite these excellences, the logic of the
Reflections is not universally convincing, and, when
Burke approached the subject once more in his letters on
the *Proposals for Peace with the Regicide Directory*, he
involved himself still further in difficulty. It was
inevitable that his magnificent philosophical grasp
should find expression in these *Proposals*. He expands,
for example, the law of civil vicinity, hinted at in the
Reflections: " As to the right of men to act anywhere
according to their pleasure, without any moral tie, no
such right exists. Men are never in a state of *total*
independence of each other." His views on war are
marked by a fine sanity : " The blood of man should
never be shed but to redeem the blood of man. It is
well shed for our family, for our friends, for our God,
for our country, for our kind. The rest is vanity; the
rest is crime," and so on. But, as in the *Reflections*,
Burke refuses to look steadily at facts. He chose to
consider the Revolution a political movement, whereas
it was a social movement. His denunciation of war
appears mere empty rhetoric, in view of the fact that,
when in 1797 the mass of the English people were
clamouring for peace, Burke was hounding on the govern-
ment to war. He denounced the new directors as
murderers and thieves, confounding Carnot and Hoche
with their allies. His anti-democratic attitude prevented
him from understanding, as men like Arthur Young
did, the real grievances of the French. Yet despite all
this, Burke remains, in Buckle's verdict, " the greatest
political thinker (Bacon excepted) who has ever devoted
himself to the practice of English politics." His style,

again, rich in metaphor and simile, and leavened by a fine humour and irony, ranks, by its lucidity and harmony, in the first order of English oratory.

In the year following the publication of the *Reflections on the French Revolution*, a humble thinker in the sphere of political philosophy, Thomas Paine, issued his *Rights of Man* (1791), in which, undaunted by the torrents of Burke's eloquence, he levelled his aim directly at the orator. Paine has no graces but much common sense. Some of his propositions had already been riddled by Burke, and others were to fall into desuetude as soon as their fallacy was detected, but Paine's arguments for the rights of the French *tiers état* were unconfuted. Paine had been abroad at the critical moment, and his account of the early stages of the Revolution was given at first hand.

The weakness of Paine's central theory was effectively laid bare by Jeremy Bentham, the pioneer of modern philosophical Radicalism. A writer, to whom poetry seemed nothing but " misrepresentation " and Burke's magnificent prose mere insanity, must needs have been heavily handicapped in the field of literature. But Bentham found his sphere in the technicalities of the law-system, and attained to such familiarity with its intricacies that the results achieved are not easily over-estimated. It has been asserted by Maine that not a single law-reform has been effected since Bentham's day, which cannot be traced to his influence.

If we set Bentham's identification of ancestral wisdom with " the infantile foolishness of the cradle of the race " alongside Burke's reverent pronouncements regarding the past, our historic sense receives somewhat of a shock. In point of fact, Bentham's historical views are void of worth. He is more himself when confronting the doctrinaire utterances of the revolutionary school and the well-aired topic of the rights of man. Bentham meets this latter with a flat negative. Man has, for him, no natural rights, since even the most cherished so-called rights—those of life and property—have grown up with the state. "Rights," he explains in a sentence, which must not be allowed to pass without reservation, "properly so-called are the creatures of law properly so-called; real laws give birth to real rights." Thus he parted company with Paine and the constitutionalists. Bentham is best remembered in the history of political thought by his formula, "the greatest happiness of the greatest number." His utilitarianism made a disciple of James Mill and through him of John Mill, and, whatever its fallacies, has proved a stimulus towards general benevolence, such as can be claimed for few other philosophical conceptions.

The beginnings of modern periodical criticism are to be found in the *Edinburgh Review*, the famous "blue and yellow" journal which began its career in October, 1802. An account of its inauguration has been left by Sydney Smith who claims the suggestion for himself. "Towards the close of my residence in Edinburgh, Brougham, Jeffrey, and myself happened to meet in the eighth or ninth story or flat, the then elevated residence of Mr. Jeffrey. I proposed that we should set up a review : this was acceded to with acclamation. I was appointed editor, and remained long enough in Edinburgh to edit the first number of the review." Sydney Smith, then, has the credit of having been the originator, though it was Jeffrey, undoubtedly, to whom the review owed its early successes, and his was the foremost of the names associated with the venture from the outset. The *Edinburgh Review* supported itself from the beginning "on two legs"; its articles, not confined to literature, dealt largely with politics—questions of Parliamentary reform, Roman Catholic emancipation, popular education, and other reform measures. The *Edinburgh* was, in short, a strenuous advocate for Whig principles and ideals. The list of names, associated with Jeffrey in the early years of the *Review's* existence, suggests that all were Whigs and young men.

Brougham, the future Whig Lord Chancellor, for many years the most voluminous of the contributors, was a writer of extraordinary versatility and unbounded confidence, strongly opposed to the slavery movement, but so inflammable that it needed all Jeffrey's resource to keep his ally in hand. Francis Horner, a young man of encyclopædic ambition, best remembered by Sydney Smith's remark that " the Ten Commandments were written on his countenance," survived only a few years, his death being regarded as a serious blow to the Whig cause. Sydney Smith, the most versatile of the wits of his day, was thirty-one at the date of the *Review's* inauguration, and Jeffrey himself twenty-nine.

The Whig character of the new journal is apparent from its literary, no less than its political, standpoint. Whiggism, with its respect for tradition, combined with an instinct for reform, stood midway between Conservatism and Radicalism. Naturally averse to mysticism, the Whig intellect looked to literature for those qualities it was most capable of appreciating—clearness and precision. But, though constitutional by instinct and opposed to theory, Whiggism was, by no means, inclined to acquiesce in the *status quo,* and the importance of the new venture lay in the fact that it proclaimed, in the face of established opinion, the pressing need for reform, whether in the sphere of politics or of letters.

The first Edinburgh reviewers failed to attain to anything like the achievement of their successors. Much of their work was perfunctory and incomplete. With youthful enthusiasm, Jeffrey and his allies ventured too far afield, failing to perceive that an organized survey, not only of literature, but of history, metaphysics, and politics, was beyond their powers. The majority of their articles have, consequently, fallen into oblivion, and, in the realm of pure letters, none of them achieved much, with the exception of Jeffrey. Sydney Smith had insufficient patience to develop into a critic, and his inborn dislike for anything approaching enthusiasm put him out of touch with contemporary movements. His best work was done outside the *Review*, though he contributed some things in his special vein. The case of Jeffrey presents peculiar difficulties, for, while he was the most competent of the circle, he displays limitations, at first sight inexplicable.

There is, first of all, the famous "This will never do!", introducing the review of Wordsworth's *Excursion* (November, 1814), side by side with the enthusiastic appreciation of Rogers and Moore. Of his contemporaries, it was, in point of fact, Campbell and Crabbe, rather than the romantics who earned Jeffrey's approbation. Again, we have the comparatively appreciative review of Keats, though this was possibly evoked by the hostility of the *Quarterly*. Byron, when he attained to fame, was handsomely received, but his first appearance had been hailed with abuse by Brougham, no doubt with Jeffrey's countenance: "Whatever judgment may be passed on this noble minor, it seems we must take them as we find them, and be content, for they are the last we shall ever have from him" (*Hours of Idleness*). Again, Jeffrey has high praise for Shakespeare, for the English classicists, and particularly for Cowper.

The essentially Whig temperament of the Edinburgh reviewers has been adduced in partial explanation. Respect for tradition serves to explain Jeffrey's attitude towards the Elizabethans and the eighteenth century classicists, while his interest in progress accounts for the championing of Cowper whose poems had been before the public eye for years. The nature study of the early romantics stood in a different position from the revolutionary mysticism of the Lakists—and Jeffrey, while he accords respect to the former, finds no difficulty in discounting the latter. Again, some explanation of Jeffrey's standpoint may be found in what Professor Saintsbury has described as the Gallican strain in his temperament. He belonged to a school, to whom the " rules " represented the guiding principles, by which literature is to be estimated. If, then, Jeffrey was sympathetic in his attitude towards older literature, he was hostile in his attitude towards the new. The dogmatism of " This will never do ! " sprang from a critical creed in keeping with that of Boileau or La Harpe. " Poetry," he wrote, " has this much, at least, in common with religion, that its standards were fixed long ago, by certain inspired writers, whose authority it is no longer lawful to question."

Yet Jeffrey's enthusiasm for the Elizabethans, whom he declares he has " long worshipped in secret with a sort of idolatrous veneration," would alone prevent us from regarding him as a thorough-going classicist. If he conforms, in general, to the code of common sense, he is prepared to surrender to his emotions, even when dealing with the moderns; if he makes the " rules " his guide, he does not hold them equally important. The triviality of his criticisms on the *Excursion* culminates in the admission that there are " a very great number of single lines and images, that sparkle like gems in the desert, and startle us by an intimation of the great poetic powers that lie buried in the rubbish that has been heaped around them," and again : " But the truth is, that Mr. Wordsworth, with all his perversities, is a person of great powers; and has frequently a force in his moral declamations, and a tenderness in his pathetic narratives, which neither his prolixity nor his affectation can altogether deprive of their effect." As for the " rules," he writes, in speaking of Byron : " For ourselves, we will confess that we have had a considerable contempt for those same *Unities*, ever since we read Dennis's *Criticism on Cato* in our boyhood—except, indeed, the unity of action, which Lord Byron does not appear to set much store by."

Certain services which Jeffrey rendered to literature must be recalled. He raised the tone of periodical literature by transforming the hack-writer into a responsible reviewer with adequate remuneration. He transformed the art of reviewing into a profession worthy of esteem, and his method set a model, which has been followed, more or less, for a century.

Brief mention may be made of a number of rival periodicals, which sprang into being soon after the appearance of the *Edinburgh*. Jeffrey's review had been conducted on principles moderate enough to permit of contributions from Sir Walter Scott, despite his Tory views. But the time came when a cleavage was inevitable, and Murray inaugurated the *Quarterly* in 1809 as a definitely Tory organ with William Gifford as editor. After Gifford, the editorship fell to Lockhart who enhanced the value of the periodical, though the review of Keats's *Endymion* (April, 1818) earned it an unenviable notoriety.

The year 1817 saw the appearance of yet a third periodical—*Blackwood's Magazine*—in which politics figured less prominently than in the two quarterlies. *Blackwood's* set itself in fierce opposition to the so-called " Cockney school " of Leigh Hunt and Keats, but was strangely appreciative of Wordsworth's work : " Whoever wishes to understand Mr. Wordsworth's philosophical opinions will find them developed in their most perfect form in the *Excursion*; but those who wish to judge merely how far he possesses the powers commonly called poetical will do best to read his *Lyrical Ballads* and smaller *Poems*, where pathos, imagination, and knowledge of human nature are often presented by themselves without any obtrusive or argumentative reference to a system. At the same time, the reverential awe and the far-extended sympathy with which he looks upon the whole system of existing things, and the silent moral connections which he supposes to exit among them are visible throughout all his writings."

X

BYRON

BYRON, Shelley, and Keats, the direct successors of Wordsworth, Coleridge, and Southey, held sway in poetry from 1816 to 1820, during which period there appeared from their pens a notable set of works— *Childe Harold* (III) and *Alastor* (1816), *Manfred* and Keats's poems of 1817, the *Revolt of Islam* and *Endymion* (1818), *Don Juan* (I and II) and the *Cenci* (1819), *Prometheus Unbound*, *Lamia*, and Keats's *Odes* (1820). Between the two groups, Campbell and Moore figured as the recognized poets.

Some interaction between the later romantic group and their predecessors must be recognized, since the debt of Shelley and Keats to Coleridge and Wordsworth was considerable. Apart from Coleridge *La Belle Dame* could scarce have been written, while *Alastor* owed much to Wordsworth. Byron learnt from Scott, and ousted him from his own field. But the early romantics had developed conservative tendencies, whereas their successors remained consistent in their revolutionary attitudes. With this second group, new influences began to bear upon the main stream of English literature, chiefly Hellenistic. On the other hand, the medieval note is less prominent than heretofore, for, despite the fact that Byron employed the Spenserian stanza in *Childe Harold* and shifted the scene of *Lara* and *Parisina* into feudal times, he was averse to mysticism. Side by side with Hellenism, a new interest in Dante, Boccaccio, and Ariosto is exemplified in both Byron and Keats, and, to some extent, in Shelley.

135

From the point of view of both heredity and environment, Fortune would appear to have frowned on Byron in his childhood. The later generations of the family had displayed propensities to violence. Left alone with his mother at the age of three, the boy might in some ways have been considered fortunate, but Mrs. Byron proved as passionate as the worst of the male lords. Pleasant must have been the scenes in the little household when the child, naturally sensitive and abused for his deformity, began to retort in self-defence. Moore tells how, one day, after a violent quarrel, both went separately to the apothecary's, " inquiring anxiously whether the other had been to purchase poison, and cautioning the vendor of drugs not to attend to such an application, if made." After varied experiences of schools Byron was sent to Harrow, where he developed passionate friendships. For regular work he showed aversion, but read voraciously. His lameness prevented him from joining in the school sports, but before he left he was recognized as a leader. At Cambridge (1805-8) he played the dandy and the sportsman, devoting time to riding, boxing, swimming, and pistol-shooting. The chief literary product of this period was the *Hours of Idleness* (1807), a series of poems, partly original, partly translated. But these scarcely rise above average juvenilia, and betray little originality. They aroused an attack in the *Edinburgh*, the sting of which rankled in Byron's mind, until he found vent for his indignation in *English Bards and Scotch Reviewers* (1809). Here Byron first revealed his powers. With the review of his first volume infecting his mind, he determined to have at all and sundry, confounding in one heterogeneous mass the school of Scottish critics and the English Lake poets. Conceived in a satirical spirit akin to that of the Augustans, the note often rings false. Yet here was an author bold enough not to be " terrified by abuse, or bullied by the reviewers," and the public enjoyed the fray. Fortunately for Byron's character, he soon made amends. Moore who had threatened him with a duel became his lifelong friend and biographer, while to Scott his reparation was ample.

In 1809 Byron set out on a "grand tour" of Europe which occupied the next two years. From Lisbon he made his way across Spain to Seville and Gibraltar, thence, via Malta, to Albania. He passed to Athens, Ephesus, and Constantinople, returning to Athens for the winter of 1810-11, and was back in England in July, 1811. *Childe Harold*, the first two cantos of which were published early in 1812, is the poetic record of this tour. One is reminded by occasional mannerisms that Addison had anticipated Byron in a verse *Letter from Italy*. But, apart from scattered reminiscences of eighteenth century diction, there is no likeness between the poems.

The romantic spirit permeating *Childe Harold*, combined with elements essentially Byronic, made the poet's reputation. "He awoke," as has often been said, "to find himself famous." Henceforth, the line of success was marked out, and, taking his cue from Scott, Byron devoted the next few years to a series of poems which ultimately drove Scott from the field. The *Giaour* (1813), the *Bride of Abydos* (1813), the *Corsair* (1814), *Lara* (1814), the *Siege of Corinth* (1816), and *Parisina* (1816) were mere revivals of the *Childe* theme with the metre changed to the more rapid measure popularized by *Marmion* and the *Lay*, or, in the case of the *Corsair* and *Lara*, with a reversion to the heroic couplet. Like *Childe Harold* the poems of 1813-16 developed round a single conception—that of the Byronic hero, in some ways an inheritance from Mrs. Radcliffe's novels, but rather an expression of the poet's individuality. In Byron's poems an age, glutted to satiety, found subject for amazement and relief. The insincerities of the Della Cruscan school were here transmuted into something new by a poet fully convinced of his own sincerity. The breath of romance plays through these poems, tinged with an Eastern or medieval colouring, beside which the rival work of Scott pales. Scott had little psychology, though he possessed the historical sense : Byron, though deficient where Scott was strong, understood himself, and, in the portraits of Harold, Lara, the Giaour and the Corsair, imposed his personality upon the public. Though these portraits present Byron in his favourite pose, he was scarcely fair to himself; the *Childe* represents him merely as he desired to be regarded. Scott, at any rate, was not deceived :

Childe Harold is, I think, a very clever poem, but gives no symptoms of the writer's heart or morals. Vice ought to be a little more modest, and it must require impudence almost equal to the noble Lord's other powers, to claim sympathy for the ennui arising from his being tired of his wassailers and his paramours. There is a monstrous deal of conceit in it, too, for it is informing the inferior part of the world that their little old-fashioned scruples of limitation are not worthy of his regard.

There can be no doubt that Byron enjoyed his new rôle. The poems consist, one and all, of a series of vivid sensations. But an unhealthy morbidity permeates them, and it is in a world of lawlessness and passion that the Byronic hero moves. Byron's style is often reminiscent of the eighteenth century, and his enthusiasm for Pope is genuine. Yet his real kinship is with the romantics, and his most striking effects resemble stage sensations. He compels enthusiasm by rhetorical devices which only the lapse of time has deprived of a measure of their appeal. The immediate sensation created by his poems is attested by the contemporary demand for them.

The crisis in Byron's life came in 1816. He had married Miss Milbanke in the previous year, but, the tempers of the pair proving incompatible, a separation took place. Society sided with the lady, and the outburst drove Byron from the country. He made his way to Geneva, where he formed the acquaintance of Shelley, the pair spending much time together on the lake. The chief products of this year were the third canto of *Childe Harold*—the last of the *Harold* series—the *Siege of Corinth, Parisina,* and the semi-historical *Prisoner of Chillon*. The later cantos of *Childe Harold* mark an advance on the sections of 1812. The description of Venice in Canto 4, the finely chiselled lines on the gladiator, together with the magnificent enthusiasm for mountain and sea, suggest the advent of a new poetry, which, if neither Wordsworthian nor Shelleian, was, at least, unexampled in its own manner.

> Thou glorious mirror, where the Almighty's form
> Glasses itself in tempests; in all time—
> Calm or convulsed, in breeze, or gale, or storm,
> Icing the pole, or in the torrid clime
> Dark-heaving—boundless, endless, and sublime,
> The image of eternity, the throne
> Of the Invisible; even from out thy slime
> The monsters of the deep are made; each zone
> Obeys thee; thou goest forth, dread, fathomless, alone.

The *Prisoner of Chillon,* inspired by that symbol of medieval tyranny, the ancient structure on the eastern border of Lac Léman, was a plea for freedom anticipatory of Byron's later exploits. A product of two rainy days at Ouchy, it serves to confirm the impression of Byron's facility.

In 1817 Byron settled in the Palazzo Mocenigo on the Grand Canal at Venice, where he wrote *Manfred* (1817), the fourth canto of *Childe Harold* (1818), *Beppo,* (1818) and parts of *Don Juan*. *Manfred* was conceived in the Swiss mountains rather than among the scenes, with which Byron became familiar in the year of its publication. The drama is laid among the high Alps, partly in Manfred's castle, partly in the mountains. In the opening scene, Manfred figures alone in a Gothic gallery at midnight—a piece of medievalism characteristic of the new romantics—and a Faust-like motif runs throughout. It was the first of a series of Byronic dramas, the majority written at Ravenna—*Marino Faliero* (1820), *Sardanapalus,* the *Two Foscari* (1821),

Cain (1821), *Werner* (1822), and the *Deformed Trans-formed* (1824). *Manfred* has been compared with *Faust*, but in a letter to Murray (June 7th, 1820) Byron denied any considerable obligations: " *Faust* I never read, for I don't know German; but Matthew Monk Lewis, in 1816, at Coligny, translated much of it to me *viva voce*, and I was naturally much struck with it; but it was the Steinbach and the Jungfrau and something else, much more than Faustus, that made me write *Manfred*." Goethe himself admitted Byron's originality: " He has made use of the impelling principles in his own way, for his own purposes, so that not one of them remains the same; and it is particularly on this account that I cannot enough admire his genius." Still, despite essential differences of conception, reminiscences of *Faust* are traceable, in spite of the fact that the central motive is " remorse, eternal suffering for inexpiable crime." Macaulay maintained that Byron's genius was essentially undramatic: " It may be doubted whether there is, in all Lord Byron's plays, a single remarkable passage, which owes any portion of its interest or effect to its connexion with the characters or the action." Hence the tendency towards soliloquy rather than dialogue, the monologues and self-communings, characteristic of both *Manfred* and *Cain*. It was the lyrical side of *Faust* which appealed chiefly to the English poet, and the aerial spirits assume a new rôle as mere figments in the mind of the protagonist:

> We answer as we answered; our reply
> Is even thine own words.
> —*Manfred*, Act i.

Again, the subjective note predominates, as in the address of the spirits in the same scene:

> By thy delight in others' pain
> And by thy brotherhood of Cain,
> I call upon thee! and compel
> Thyself to be thy proper hell,

or the passage at the close:

> The mind which is immortal makes itself
> Requital for its good or evil thoughts,
> Is its own origin of ill and end
> And its own place and time: its innate sense,
> When stripp'd of this mortality, derives
> No colour from the fleeting things without,
> But is absorbed in sufferance or in joy,
> Born from the knowledge of its own desert.

In *Cain*, Byron's dramatic masterpiece, there is somewhat closer contact with the world of fact, for, while Cain's struggle remains subjective, his tragic fall is definitely related to the death of Abel. The lyrical element, exemplified in *Manfred* by the eloquent apostrophe to the sun, gains added pathos from its association with Cain's sister, Zillah, his wife, and child. There is no proof that Byron derived anything from Gessner's *Death of Abel* which he had not read since childhood. His general impression was one of pleasure, but of details he had only shadowy recollections. In *Marino Faliero* and the *Two Foscari* his themes were Italian, though German influence reappeared in *Werner* and the *Deformed Transformed*.

At Venice Byron had tried his hand on a new poem, in which the dominant elements were to be humour and satire. This was *Beppo*, a Venetian story, written in imitation of Frere's *Whistlecraft* (1817), in which *ottava rima* and a pseudo-Arthurian framework had served as a vehicle for wit and burlesque:

> They looked a manly generous generation,
>   Beards, shoulders, eyebrows, broad and square and thick,
> Their accents firm and loud in conversation,
>   Their eyes and gestures eager, sharp and quick,
> Shewed them prepared on proper provocation
>   To give the lie, pull noses, stab and kick;
> And for that very reason it is said,
> They were so very courteous and well-bred.

Beppo constitutes a *Don Juan* in little, and its success led Byron to the composition of the longer poem. But, before the completion of the latter, Byron was to pass through many experiences. He had made the acquaintance of the Countess Teresa Guicciofi in 1819: the acquaintance ripened on both sides into a passion, and Byron followed her to Ravenna which remained his headquarters until the close of 1821. Here he composed his *Prophecy of Dante* (1821) and the *Vision of Judgment* (1823). The *Prophecy of Dante* (1821) was an attempt to realize the significance of Dante for modern thought and an experiment in *terza rima*. Its note of regret is characteristic of the exile:

> An exile, saddest of all prisoners,
> Who has the whole world for a dungeon strong,
> Seas, mountains, and the horizon's verge for bars,
> Which shut him from the sole small spot of earth,
> Where—whatsoe'er his fate—he still were hers,
> His country's, and might die where he had birth.

But the *Prophecy* does not represent Byron's dominant mood, for which we must look elsewhere, to the *Vision of Judgment* (1823) and *Don Juan* (1824).

Byron had not succeeded in handling *terza rima* with conspicuous success, and in the *Vision* and its successor he had recourse to his most effective instrument, *ottava rima*. The *Vision of Judgment* proved an overwhelming retort to Southey's " Satanic School " and his servile flattery of George III. In his Preface, Southey had described Byron and his followers as|

> Men of diseased hearts and depraved imaginations who, forming a system of opinions to suit their own unhappy course of conduct, have rebelled against the holiest ordinances of human society, and, hating that revealed religion which, with all their efforts and bravadoes, they are unable entirely to disbelieve, labour to make others as miserable as themselves by infecting them with a moral virus that eats into the soul.

Byron's retort took the form of a satire not only of Southey but of his royal idol. St. Peter sits listlessly outside the gates of heaven. Then follows the funeral of George III and the summoning of Wilkes, as one of Satan's cloud of witnesses:

> " Some,"
> Said Wilkes, " don't wait to see them laid in lead,

For such a liberty—and I, for one,
Have told them what I thought beneath the sun.''

Junius appears as second witness, but is unable to produce any new evidence, whereupon Southey himself is dragged in by Asmodeus. The assembly comes to a sudden termination with Southey's offer to recite his poem.

Don Juan, extending to sixteen cantos and lacking a definite plot, cannot be described simply. It represents Byron in his maturity and under every aspect. The tone is both mocking and serious, a compound of irreverence and flippancy, permeated by the qualities foreshadowed in *Childe Harold*. A medley of sardonic humour, witty reflection, and intense denunciation, composed under an Italian sky, it gives expression to views not easily acceptable to an English audience. *Don Juan* represents the death-blow of convention, romanticism submitting to self-analysis :

> 'Tis melancholy, and a fearful sign
>   Of human frailty, folly, also crime,
> That love and marriage rarely can combine,
>   Although they both are born in the same clime;
> Marriage from love, like vinegar from wine—
> A sad, sour, sober beverage—by time
> Is sharpened from its high celestial flavour,
> Down to a very homely household savour.

At Ravenna Byron interested himself in revolutionary Italian politics. His thoughts turned to Greece, and in 1823 he sailed from Genoa to Cephalonia. His chief difficulties arose from his allies, and, after months of energetic action, he contracted a fever in the swamps at Missolonghi, and died on April 19th, 1824.

Byron had been in the neighbourhood of Pisa at the date of Shelley's death (1822). Leigh Hunt had just arrived in Italy with the object of securing Shelley's assistance in the production of a new journal, but the death of Shelley led Hunt to Byron. After Byron's death Hunt wrote an unfavourable account of Byron, to which Moore replied. Though much of what Hunt had to say may have been true, publication was another matter. To estimate Byron's character is, in any case, difficult, in view of his love of pose and isolation. From his *Letters* and conversation he appears to have been fundamentally honest, however much he may have masqueraded under a veil of affectation. " *Don Juan*," he wrote, " is too true, and would, I suspect, live longer than *Childe Harolde*. The women hate many things which strip off the tinsel of sentiment." The active life attracted him, first and foremost, and he scorned to be reckoned a mere poet. Liberty was ever his ideal, and, in pursuit of this, he displayed much abnegation. An interesting account of Byron, as he impressed one observer, has been handed down by Trelawney, who represents him as extremely vivacious and much addicted to sport. His triumph was to have swum the Hellespont from Sestos to Abydos. His dawdling habits also impressed his biographer, together with his abstemiousness, which seems to have been dictated by the fear of becoming stout. He would exist for days on biscuits and soda-water. When he set out for Greece, Trelawney accompanied him, and left an interesting account of Byron's daily life, the dives over the vessel's side, and the shooting matches with pistols.

Byron's place in literature is not easy to determine. Assuredly a master-type, he has been more popular abroad than any English poet, and Goethe described him as the greatest genius of his age. Without a trace of insularity, his influence has been European. In Russia, Germany, Spain, and France, *le Byronisme*, *der Byronismus*, or whatever name it assumed, proved the chief romantic force of the century.

But Matthew Arnold fell foul of Byron's style in the *Essays on Criticism*, and it is impossible to defend lapses like

There let him lay,

or the proverbial slovenliness of his blank verse. Swinburne went further, describing his style as " jolter-

headed jargon," but made amends by emphasizing the
" splendid imperishable excellence, which covers all his
offences and outweighs all his defects : the excellence
of sincerity and strength." But Byron recognized his
own limitations. " Mrs. Shelley," he once remarked,
" demurs at my grammar and spelling. I am in good
company, Cromwell and Napoleon, they were careless
of grammar, but careful of the matter; so am I." His
popularity was due to his splendid daring and many-
sidedness, and he wins a permanent place in literature
by his genuine poetry, his witty persiflage, and his
contempt for all forms of sham :

> He taught us little; but our soul
> Had *felt* him like the thunder's roll.
> With shivering heart the strife we saw
> Of passion with eternal law;
> And yet with reverential awe
> We watch'd the fount of fiery life
> Which served for that Titanic strife.

XI

KEATS

THE representatives of the younger school of romantic-
ism—Byron, Shelley, and Keats—were sufficiently
individualistic to suggest in each case the need for
differentiation. If, in Byron, the romantic note took
the form of moody self-consciousness, in Shelley of
revolutionary idealism, the fundamental conception in
Keats was that of beauty for beauty's sake. To trace
the development of this artistic faith becomes a matter
of engrossing interest to Keats's biographer, the material
lying to hand in the poems and letters.

Keats's early environment might easily have been
pronounced unfavourable for poetic production. The
combination of factors necessary for the development
of literary genius is not, however, readily ascertainable,
apart from the fact that one may easily undervalue the
particular combination that produced Keats. His father
was, undoubtedly, a young man of parts, since he
ultimately married his master's daughter, and took over
the charge of the livery business. His mother appears
to have possessed talent and sense, in addition to a
handsome face : she was passionately attached to her
eldest son who reciprocated her affection.

At the age of nine Keats lost his father who
sustained a fracture of the skull owing to a fall from
his horse. At this date Keats was in school at Enfield,
where he made the acquaintance, destined to be life-
long, of Charles Cowden Clarke, the schoolmaster's
son. As a child Keats had shown signs of impetuosity,
which, at school, displayed itself in a penchant for

146

fighting. His disposition was marked by both pugnacity and generosity, tears alternating with fits of laughter, but "associated as they were with an extraordinary beauty of person and expression, these qualities captivated the boys, and no one was more popular." Charles Cowden Clarke, to whom we owe the most important record of these years, declares that the passion for literature developed in Keats during the last year or so of his schooling: "In my mind's eye I now see him at supper (we had our meals in the schoolroom) sitting back on the form, from the table, holding the folio volume of Burnet's *History of Our Own Time* between himself and the table, eating his meal from beyond it." Keats progressed with Latin and French, but never acquired Greek : his knowledge of classical mythology was derived from Chapman's *Homer*, the Elizabethans, and the uninspired Lemprière of Cowden Clarke's list.

Keats's mother died in 1810, and her loss proved so overwhelming that the boy would hide himself in despair under the schoolmaster's desk; the sensibility characteristic of the poet throughout life was already abnormally developed. His apprenticeship to surgery, however, left but fleeting impressions on his mind. He had abundant leisure, and, in 1814, is described by Cowden Clarke as making his first acquaintance with the *Faerie Queene*, which he went through " as a young horse thro' a spring meadow, ramping." Appropriately, his first poem was entitled an *Imitation of Spenser*. (1817)

It was not long before Keats, now a medical student in the London hospitals, made the acquaintance of Haydon and Leigh Hunt—determining factors in his choice of a literary career. The latter has left an account of his first meeting with Keats in 1816: " We read and walked together, and used to write verses of an evening upon a given subject. No imaginative pleasure was left unnoticed by us, or unenjoyed; from the recollection of the bards and patriots of old, to the luxury of a summer rain at our window, or the clicking of the coal in winter-time.''

Keats's first volume (1871), inscribed with a quotation from Spenser's *Muiopotmos*,

> What more felicity can fall to creature
> Than to enjoy delight with liberty,

was dedicated, in verse, to Leigh Hunt. The influence of much reading among the poets—Spenser, Chapman, Browne, Chatterton—combined with Hunt's all-pervading influence, is apparent throughout. The diction, both luscious and familiar, and the loose rhythm of *Rimini* reappear in Keats's volume. But the descriptive passages are marked by an extraordinary poetic sensibility, and there are numerous indications of the future direction of Keats's genius. The loose verse-structure contrasts startlingly with that of eighteenth century classical poets, and is reminiscent of Chamberlayne in the seventeenth. As a whole, the volume betrays a lack of artistic control and an over-exuberance of fancy, while the rhymes seem frequently forced :

> And now the sharp keel of his little boat
> Comes up with ripple and with easy float.
> —*Calidore*

> Those marble steps that through the water dip,
> Now over them he goes with hearty trip.
> —*Calidore*

There is, besides, an occasional use of familiar terms, such as Hunt had practised, but, by no means, justified : e.g.

> what amorous and fondling nips
> They gave each other's cheeks.

Though this early venture met with no appreciation from the public at large, it was complimented in the *Champion* (March, 1817) and the *European Magazine* (May, 1817), while Hunt, as in duty bound, noticed it in his *Examiner*, discriminating between its strong and weak points. In some of the poems he detected '' an exquisite proof of close observation of nature as well as the most luxuriant fancy," but observed that Keats " wants age for a greater knowledge of humanity, though evidences of this also bud forth here and there." But it is precisely in the evidences that " bud forth here and there " that the charm of the volume consists —the magic of the single line, side by side with the few poems, in which the artistry is maintained from end to end. The supreme example is, no doubt, the sonnet *On first looking into Chapman's Homer*, where the rigid verse-form seems to compel restraint. Less distinguished in conception, though exquisite as an expression of luxuriant fancy based on Greek mythology, is the dedicatory sonnet, while the lines to Georgiana Augusta Wylie provide the happiest example of skill in octosyllables :

> Hadst thou lived in days of old,
> O what wonders had been told
> Of thy lovely countenance,
> And thy humid eyes that dance
> In the midst of their own brightness,
> In the very fane of lightness.

Apart from such accomplished examples, there are indications of Keats's growing conception of his art— confidential in the *Epistles* to his brother and to Cowden Clarke, and rising to a note of triumph in *Sleep and Poetry*. The attack on eighteenth century style, which suggested to Courthope the over-assurance of a young man not yet arrived at an historic estimate of literature, is, after all, but the climax of the attacks on artificialism, inaugurated by Cowper. The bold prophecy of future accomplishment was destined, in any case, to be completely fulfilled.

It was in February, 1817, that Keats first met Shelley, introduced by Leigh Hunt. According to the latter, Keats was a little over-sensitive on the score of his origin, and " inclined to see in every man of birth a sort of natural enemy." The methods of the pair were, indeed, opposed, Keats having little sympathy with the social theories, with which Shelley was ingrained. But they were on sufficiently good terms to arrange a kind of competition—the production of rival poems to be completed within six months. Shelley's *Revolt of Islam* appeared within the stipulated time, but *Endymion* was delayed till the winter of 1817-18. This latter, described on the title-page as " A Poetic Romance," and bearing a motto from Shakespeare's seventeenth sonnet, " The stretched metre of an antique song," was dedicated " to the memory of Chatterton," according to an earlier version " the most English of poets except Shakespeare." The Preface is a plea for consideration in view of the poet's immaturity, the subject the Greek story of the moon-goddess, Cynthia, and her love for the Cretan youth, Endymion. Yet the poem itself is but half-Greek, the key-note being the passionate thirst for beauty of a modern romantic. Keats's " exquisite sense of the luxurious," his voluptuous and effeminate style, produces at times an almost cloying effect, and its weak points were, naturally, seized upon by the hostile reviewers of *Blackwood's* and the *Quarterly*. But Keats himself had ascribed to *Endymion* " every error denoting a feverish attempt rather than a deed accomplished," and the legend that his early death was directly due to criticism is an invention. " 'Tis strange," said Byron,

> 'Tis strange, the mind, that very fiery particle,
> Should let itself be snuffed out by an article,

but the true point of view was put by Keats himself in a letter of October, 1818 : My own criticism has given me pain " beyond what *Blackwood* or the *Quarterly* could possibly inflict; and also, when I feel I am right, no external praise can give me such a glow as my own solitary reperception and ratification of what is fine." Some of the strictures in the reviews were, no doubt, justified, but the contemptuous tone of the attacks remains a discredit to criticism. The blindness of the reviewers, when it became a question of real achievement, is astounding. The *Hymn to Pan*, described by Wordsworth as a " very pretty piece of paganism," the " roundelay " on Bacchus, the account of things primeval in Book III, or the lines replete with a sense of mystery,

> He ne'er is crown'd
> With immortality, who fears to follow
> Where airy voices lead—

these things evoked no enthusiasm, and suggested no future achievement. *Endymion* reveals a Keats still in his apprenticeship, but an apprenticeship, of which he had already thrown off many of the shackles. That he was already conscious of the need for restraint is clear from his revisions, illustrated by the marvellous re-shaping of

> A thing of beauty is a constant joy

into

> A thing of beauty is a joy for ever,

and so throughout.

The rapidity, with which Keats attained his maturity, is attested by the fact that *Isabella* was already in hand during the early months of 1818, while *Hyperion*, the *Eve of St. Agnes*, *Lamia*, the *Odes*, the chief sonnets, *La Belle Dame sans Merci*, and the fragment of the *Eve of St. Mark* were completed by the close of 1819.

Hyperion was begun, perhaps, at his brother's bedside, the *Ode on a Grecian Urn* during the snow-laden spring that followed upon the winter of 1818. His own disease, accentuated during these months, was scarcely benefitted by the passion he developed for Miss Brawne. To save his life, Keats was advised to spend the winter abroad. He died at Rome on the 23rd February, 1821.

Keats's third and last volume appeared in 1820, and contained, besides *Lamia*, *Isabella*, and the *Eve of St. Agnes*, the five *Odes* and the fragment of *Hyperion*.

The germ of *Lamia* was derived from the *Anatomy of Melancholy*, which Keats followed closely, but in accordance with romantic principles. The mannerisms of the early poems have not as yet disappeared—double-barrelled adjectives, " cirque-couchant," " vermilion-spotted," " rubious-argent," " milder-mooned," verbal coinages like " neighboured," " passioned," and occasional lapses in versification :

> Of all these bereft
> Nothing but pain and ugliness were left.
> Still shone her crown; that vanished, also she
> Melted and disappeared as suddenly.

But, as an example of romantic method, *Lamia* is supreme in the pictorial representation of the super-natural. The initial description of the serpent,

> She was a gordian shape of dazzling hue,
> Vermilion-spotted, golden, green, and blue;
> Striped like a zebra, freckled like a pard,
> Ey'd like a peacock, and all crimson barred,

stands out in striking contrast with that of the serpent transformed,

> There she stood
> About a young bird's flutter from a wood,
> Fair, on a sloping green of mossy tread,
> By a clear pool, wherein she passioned,
> To see herself escaped from so sore ills,
> While her robes flaunted with the daffodils,

and still more with that vivid piece of actuality drawn from the sea-coast near Corinth :

> Now on the moth-time of that evening dim
> He would return that way, as well she knew,
> To Corinth from the shore; for freshly blew
> The eastern soft wind, and his galley now
> Grated the quaystones with her brazen prow
> In port Cenchreas, from Egina isle
> Fresh anchored.

The close link between the Keats of the *Letters* and the Keats of romance is revealed by the intrusion of the critical spirit at different stages of the narrative, and the significance of his recent study of Dryden in the metrical scheme, which, while permitting of enjambment, betrays a general strengthening of the verse-line and a happy employment of alexandrines.

Isabella or the Pot of Basil was completed before *Lamia* in June, 1818. This versification of a story from the *Decamerone* arose out of an agreement between Keats and Reynolds, according to which each was to prepare a number of versified tales for a joint publication. Reynolds's contributions consisted of the *Garden of Florence* and the *Lady of Provence*. The story selected by Keats, Boccaccio's fifth novel of the fourth day, gains an added beauty in his hands despite its inherent difficulty. The lively contrast between the brothers and Lorenzo is due to Keats, though the lack of a precedent in the original aroused his timidity. Again, Boccaccio's hint, conveyed to Isabella in a dream: " ' My dear Isabel, thou grievest incessantly for my absence, and art continually calling upon me; but know that I can return no more to thee, for the last day that thou sawest me, thy brothers put me to death,' and, describing the place where they had buried him, he bid her call no more upon him,'' is transformed into the romantic description of the grave shadowed by beeches and chestnuts, near which sheep bleat and bees murmur. The concluding stanzas constitute a modern variant of Boccaccio's closing lines :

" But, in some time afterwards, the thing became public, which gave rise to this song:

'Most cruel and unkind was he
That of my flowers deprived me.' "

The *Eve of St. Agnes*, begun, according to Lord Houghton, on a visit to Hampshire early in 1819, was finished on Keats's return to Hampstead. Together with the *Eve of St. Mark* it represents a revolt and temporary relaxation from the austerity of Milton, in rivalry with whom Keats had been fitfully planning his epic, *Hyperion*. Its warm romantic colouring, its embroidery, and medieval trappings, associated with the quiet theme of " love and winged St. Agnes's saintly care," assured the triumph of this essay in pictorial art. The kaleidoscopic changes from the opening scene with its frozen beadsman and frozen world to the revelry and passion of the hall, on to the solitude of the chamber, where Madeline sleeps,

> Flown, like a thought, until the morrow-day,
> Blissfully haven'd both from joy and pain,
> Clasp'd like a missal where swart Paynims pray,
> Blinded alike from sunshine and from rain,
> As though a rose should shut, and be a bud again,

exemplify the method of pictorial contrast. The delicately-sketched portrait of Madeline herself,

> Hoodwink'd with faery fancy, all amort,
> Save to St. Agnes and her lambs unshorn,

in contrast with the " palsy-stricken churchyard " beldame, laughing in the " languid moon," suggests similarity of method. But the story belongs clearly to " the lap of legends old," and ends with the lovers " fled away in the storm," the old nurse and beadsman dead, and the castle surrendered to the " be-night-mared " baron and his warrior-guests.

The fragmentary *Eve of St. Mark*, a piece of even more delicately chiselled medievalism, is actuated once more by the life of a saint. The affection of the " maiden fair " for her gold-embroidered volume with its

> Martyrs in a fiery blaze,
> Azure saints in silver rays,

recalls the clapped missal of the companion poem, while the " crow-quill " annotations at the foot of the text,

> Als writith he of swevenis,
> Men han beforne they wake in bliss,
> Whanne that hir friendes thinke hem bound
> In crimped shroud farre under grounde,

serve to recall Keats's indebtedness to Chatterton for at least one aspect of his medievalism.

Keats's development as an artist, suggested by the contrast between *Endymion* and *Hyperion*, was largely due to his clearer insight into the methods of Milton. His early poems suggest the Milton of the Horton period, in his later work his models were *Paradise Lost* and *Paradise Regained*, though the Elizabethan colouring of the Horton poems led Keats in a somewhat different direction. Again, the melancholy of *Il Penseroso* gains an added tinge in the hands of a poet so prone to introspection as Keats, whose hold upon life was immeasurably deepening. " If the *Hyperion* be not grand poetry," wrote Shelley, " none has been produced by our contemporaries," and tributes to its austerity and classic beauty were accorded by contemporaries. In the *Odes*, the sense of form appears side by side with a note of regret, characteristic of Keat's last period, and suggesting the influence of harsh experience. It is no longer possible, bearing in mind the standpoint of these poems and the abundant material of the *Letters*, to conceive of Keats as a mere exponent of art for art's sake. The thought of pain lingering at the heart of pleasure, expressed so poignantly in the last stanza of the *Ode on Melancholy*,

> She dwells with Beauty—Beauty that must die;
> And Joy, whose hand is ever at his lips
> Bidding Adieu; and aching Pleasure nigh,
> Turning to poison while the bee-mouth sips,

finds frequent expression in the *Letters*, e.g., " Health and spirits can only belong unalloyed to the selfish man," " Do you not see how necessary a world of pains and troubles is to school an Intelligence and make it a soul ? "

Surveying Keats's development as revealed here, the stress laid at the outset of his career on pure sensation seems to emerge into an appreciation of another force at the heart of joy. As Dr. Bradley put it, Keats supplies his own answer to the question

> And can I ever bid these joys farewell?

in the immediately following lines

> Yes, I must pass them for a nobler life,
> Where I may find the agonies, the strife
> Of human hearts,

and if Keats remains the poet of Beauty, it is a Beauty the method of attaining which he hinted at in the extraordinary illustration : " If a sparrow come before my window, I take part in its existence and pick about the gravel." Many misconceptions as to his character are removed in the course of a reading of the *Letters*. We find ourselves in the presence of an acute intellect, which has not only reflected on the problems of art, but contributed in passing to the literature of criticism, a humorous temperament not above sporting with literary material, and reasonable enough to be interested in life, in all its phases. In an early letter (May 16th, 1817) Keats amuses himself with the terminology of chivalry —the actual material of *Calidore*.

> I am extremely indebted to you for your liberality in the shape of manufactured rag, value £20, and shall immediately proceed to destroy some of the minor heads of that hydra the Dun; to conquer which the knight need have no Sword, Shield, Cuirass, Cuisses, Herbadgeon, Spear, Casque, Greaves, Paldrons, Spurs, Chevron, or any other scaly commodity, but he need only take the Bank-note of Faith and Cash of Salvation, and set out against the monster, invoking the aid of no Archimago or Urganda, but finger me the paper, light as the Sybil's leaves in Virgil, whereat the fiend skulks off with his tail between his legs. Touch him with this enchanted paper, and he whips you his head away as fast as a snail's horn—but then the horrid propensity he has to put it up again has discouraged many very valiant Knights. He is such a never-ending still-beginning sort of a body, like my landlady of the Bell. I should conjecture that the very spright that " the green sour ringlets makes Whereof the ewe not bites " had manufactured it of the dew fallen on said sour ringlets. I think I could make a nice little allegorical poem, called " The Dun," where we would have the Castle of Carelessness, the Drawbridge of Credit, Sir Novelty Fashion's expedition against the City of Tailors, etc., etc.

He is capable of punning and general frivolity (letter to Jane Reynolds, September, 1817), even of nonsense verse. (July 2nd, 1818.) His remarks on contemporaries suggest that Keats was under no misconception as to his own achievement : his criticisms are independent and without reserve. Boldly identifying the epithet " Wordsworthian " with the " egoistical sublime," he records that " Wordsworth has left a bad impression wherever he visited in town by his egotism, vanity and bigotry." Of Lamb he tells an amusing story how, at Kingston's house, " Lamb got tipsy and blew up Kingston, proceeding so far as to take the candle across the room, hold it to his face, and show us what a soft fellow he was." But Keats's mind was fundamentally serious and his critical *dicta*, whether in poems or letters, prove the truth of his brother's statement : " John was the very soul of courage and manliness, and as much like the Holy Ghost as Johnny Keats." The *dicta* in the *Letters* illustrate Keats's critical evolution from the more or less captious denunciation of " musty laws lined out with wretched rule and compass vile " in *Sleep and Poetry* to the creative judgment of the letter to Benjamin Bailey (November 22nd, 1817) : " What the imagination seizes as Beauty must be Truth—whether it existed before or not—for I have the same idea of all our passions as of Love; they are all, in their sublime, creative of essential Beauty," or again, " I think poetry should surprise by a fine excess, and not by singularity; it should strike the reader as a wording of his own highest thoughts and appear almost a remembrance." (February 27th, 1818.)

XII

SHELLEY

IT seems likely that, apart from other causes, distaste for anything approaching romantic idealism would have effectually prevented his contemporaries from appreciating Shelley's work. The canons of criticism, as expounded by the Scottish school, had found expression in the motto, *Judex damnatur cum nocens absolvitur.* Keats, arraigned before this tribunal, was declared guilty of heresy, and directed to return to his gallipots. Wordsworth succeeded in defying the gibes of his critics, but at the expense of his reputation. On the other hand, Byron, the most popular poet of his age, opened his career in the orthodox manner by paying homage to the sovereignty of Pope. It was unlikely, therefore, that an age which found itself out of sympathy with Wordsworth and Keats would be in the least degree capable of appreciating the imagery of *Alastor* or the music of the *Revolt of Islam.*

The romantic school has, in the struggle for life, gained on the classic, and the nineteenth century gave its verdict for the new canons. Of this school Shelley was the highest type and product, the complete antithesis of Pope. The limitations of neo-classical wisdom were never more tersely expressed than in the epigrammatic couplet of the *Essay on Man* :

> Know then thyself, presume not God to scan,
> The proper study of mankind is man.

With this text Pope, the high priest of his age, opened his memorable sermon on the social animal, and rising by balanced epithets to the height of his theme, brought his discourse to a conclusion with a pronouncement on humanity as

The glory, jest, and riddle of the world.

Shelley's *Triumph of Life* embodies a new attitude towards man and nature. Its note is individual, imaginative, unconventional : in a word, it is lyrical, and lyricism gives its charter to a new philosophy. In such a poem as this, a whole of sublime effect beyond the reach of painting and like to some dim unsubstantial vision of faery, there are definite component parts. The substance may, accordingly, be analysed, and the stuff, from which the fabric has been woven, viewed in the raw material.

A poet is not made but born, yet, paradoxically, the romantic element in Shelley was the direct outcome of those separate movements, pioneered by the Lake poets and the Elizabethans. The philosophy of the poems, on the other hand, embodied the results of previous speculations on law and society, and may not be fathered on his poetic ancestry. Transmuted in the current of Shelley's imagination, the stuff of these doctrines, philosophic and romantic, came out renewed, and his teachers found themselves confronted with their own weapons. Wordsworth and Coleridge, who had long since seceded from the revolutionaries, now found a pupil, who clung to the old faith and cheered on the rule of anarchy. Godwin, the calm intellectualist, begot in Shelley a disciple only too advanced in his creed, whose enthusiasm led him to indulge in experiments at the expense of his teacher. Other forces which went to the making of the poet were European, and, in that titanic revolution which shook the West, Shelley resembles the sunlight breaking through the clouds, massed on the coasts of France.

But to account for the sum-total which is a poet by elements wholly external is impossible. It is the individual element in Shelley, which eludes criticism and evades definition. That he has a mission to perform is part of every poet's creed. Keat's lines glow with this conviction, a soul's self-revelation :

> O for ten years that I may overwhelm
> Myself in poesy: so I may do the deed
> That my own soul has to itself decreed.

To dedicate himself formally to the services of Beauty and Liberty had been an act of Shelley's youth, and the ceremony finds record in two memorable passages. His early declaration at the altar of Liberty, " I will be wise and just and free and mild," finds fuller expression in the stanzas of the *Revolt of Islam*: his self-dedication to Beauty is re-emphasized in the great lines of the *Hymn to Intellectual Beauty*. Thus, at the age of sixteen, Shelley became a votary of a new religion, whose tenets found expression in the thumb-worn motto— Liberty, Fraternity, and Equality : the passwords of the French Revolution had been adopted by the adherent of a newer faith. With less definite avowal he continued to assert his loyalty to Love and Beauty, destined to be, henceforward, the dominant principles in his life.

At both Field Place and Eton, Shelley had surrounded himself with a world of phantoms and spirits. Mastery over the elusive forces of nature was to him a source of delight, but it was his visionary rather than scientific powers that he bewildered with glimpses of an impalpable world. With something of that mysticism characteristic of Blake and Wordsworth his mind turned passionately towards nature. Of necessity, such a spirit must be romantic, for the essence of romance consists in sympathy with the fears and joys that compose man's oldest inheritance. To a Johnson the surroundings of a Fleet Street may mean little more than printing-presses and copy : to a Stevenson they are instinct with forces, the possibilities of a human soul —a Dr. Jekyll and Mr. Hyde. To Shelley romanticism brought in its train a vivid sensation of life. As to the men of Asia in *Prometheus*, existence was to him

That maddening wine of life, whose dregs men drain
To deep intoxication.

The heart of a child beats in this zest of living, and to Shelley the joys that gather round childhood ever clung. Regarded across the vista of a century, this child of nature has seemed to many the spirit of poetry itself, clad in some visionary form. The Shelley of history was far other than this. As to his boon companions of the Mermaid Shakespeare was but " our pleasant Willy," so to Hogg and Peacock and Leigh Hunt Shelley was no phantom, but a mortal with feet of clay. In those delicate novels, which connoisseurs try on their palates with the relish of an epicure, Peacock's satire cuts like a knife at the weaknesses of the poet, and more than one portrait has been handed down, sketched with telling irony.

With the artistic aspect of Shelley's mind was associated a philosophic scheme which had an important bearing on his work. The Eton days had first made him acquainted with *Political Justice,* and he had immediately subscribed to its tenets. The time was not unfavourable for revolutionary doctrine, and the new moral philosophy found a notable body of adherents. Human perfectibility, the dream of French speculators, found in Shelley an eager propagandist, but it was his introduction to Godwin that finally assured him in his creed. The preachers of the French Revolution entitled their programme " A Return to Nature," and to this Godwin's originality could add little. His bald and disinterested treatment made him, however, the leader of the English school. " Give to a state liberty enough," he wrote, " and it is impossible that vice should exist in it." Law and society he condemned in favour of a social compact; individual freedom from the chains of government he hailed, as heralding the dawn of a new era; marriage was an institution fatal to society, and government a form of tyranny. Such were the doctrines handed by the thinker to the poet to form the framework of the new poetry. In their crude forms they are rarely detectable in Shelley : ingrained in the texture of his romance, they assume novel shapes and the colour of the poetic spirit.

Shelley's earliest poems, composed when his artistic touch was less sure, exhibit the welding of the parts, the speculative and the imaginative. In *Queen Mab* (1813) these fit badly. The naked soul of Ianthe " instinct with inexpressible beauty and grace," quitting the body for aerial flights, may, indeed, be regarded as a symbol of the poet's soul, but the speculative dogmas of the Fairy Mab are out of harmony with their environment and jar upon the ear. Scarcely more inspired than in their first presentment in *Political Justice*, the new theories on Law, Monarchy, and the State reappear in *Queen Mab*. Some kinship with Goldsmith may be detected in the new social economy, but, whereas the author of the *Deserted Village* preferred the limits of the heroic couplet,

> Ill fares the land to hastening ills a prey
> Where wealth accumulates and men decay,

the poet of *Queen Mab* embodies his protest in blank verse.

These purely social heresies are hardly likely to trouble a sophisticated age : Shelley's religious views have been less lightly tolerated. A tract, published at Oxford, led to the expulsion under college seal of both Shelley and Hogg. That the poet had long carried on a single-handed warfare with Calvin's school is certain from internal evidence. Carrying into all spheres his theory of individual freedom, he had been led to tilt against current doctrine, and often with the unwisdom of youth. But Shelley's attitude in *Queen Mab* was not that of the mature poet. His reverent sympathy with fundamental religious doctrine is apparent in his *Essay on Christianity*, and that closing stanza of *Adonais*, in which he embodies his conception of ideal love :

> That sustaining Love,
> Which through the web of being blindly wove
> By man and beast and earth and air and sea,
> Burns bright or dim, as each are mirrors of
> The fire for which all thirst, now beams on me
> Consuming the last clouds of cold mortality.

It is to his social, no less than his philosophical creed, that we must look for an explanation of the peculiar views, formulated in the *Epipsychidion* (1821). To Godwin legal marriage had seemed an impropriety, a fetter for binding indissolubly inharmonious natures. Shelley, to whom philosophy afforded a mere framework for poetic pageantry, erected on this background the enchanted scenery of *Epipsychidion* and his conception of true union.

Another heresy, styled the "Pythagorean," was ardently championed at Oxford, where Hogg was wont to find but meagre fare, and continued in vogue during the first wanderings over England. Milton had countenanced it in *Paradise Lost*, and Eve's reception of Raphael might have been taken as a classic precedent. Occasionally, Peacock's gibes produced a relaxation in this dietary, but the theory acquired intellectual sanction and assumed poetic form. The imaginative youth in *Alastor* makes his meal on "bloodless food," and in the *Revolt of Islam* the fruit of the earth is the staple diet of Laon and Cythna.

While Shelley ardently championed such heresies, and revealed his true nature by paying Godwin's debts, he was training his powers in another direction by long apprenticeship to his art. The days at Oxford, when Hogg would listen for the footsteps of Shelley crossing the quadrangle of New College, were memorable in his early history. On alternate nights Hogg would drop in on Shelley, to find him, as often as not, asleep before a blazing fire. Study was the chief recreation of the pair, and recollections of evenings, when Shelley would read with spirit and passion from Wordsworth or Byron, in a voice which to the ear of the Ettrick shepherd seemed "tuned in sharp fourths," occur in Hogg's writings. The Wordsworthian influence, combined with elements wholly Shelleian, appears most prominently in *Alastor* (1816)—a study in blank verse under a Greek title due to Peacock.

Since the appearance of the *Lyrical Ballads* English poetry had retreated with Wordsworth to the hills of Cumberland, or rioted with Byron through Spain and Greece. With Shelley, a new nature—

> Where the red volcano overcanopies
> The fields of snow and pinnacles of ice,
> With burning smoke; or where bitumen lakes
> On black bare pointed islets ever beat
> With sluggish surge—

a nature, familiar only to the poet's imagination, sprang into being. This new conception of nature, with something of that sympathy for the sights and sounds of "earth and ambient air," which the world learnt from Wordsworth, was the main force that produced *Alastor*. It embodies the passion of a youth for the ideal principle of Beauty—a phantom of loveliness hovering in the brain only to elude the grasp of the pursuer—and the visionary quality of Shelley's genius is, throughout, apparent. For him, as for Plato, the imagination creates for itself images, which are, in the highest sense, realities, and of these nature and humanity tend to be mere reflections. The *Revolt of Islam* (1818), passing before our eyes in a series of vignettes on the Spenserian model, hurries us from the great world struggle of eagle and serpent through the enchanted palaces of a supernatural scenery in an unwearied pursuit of these evanescent powers.

During the composition of the *Revolt* a new influence came into Shelley's life, and in company with Peacock the winter at Marlowe passed in a "mere Atticism." A study of the Greeks, systematically, begun under the direction of the novelist, had laid in Shelley's mind the foundation of a great dramatic scheme, culminating later in the fully developed

Prometheus. In the woods of Windsor or in the bottom of a boat under the open sky Shelley was, at the same time, shaping the stanzas he combined into the harmonious whole of the *Revolt of Islam.* The heroic sentiment of the *Faerie Queene* is sufficiently apparent, and imparts charm to the opening section.

In 1818, two years after Byron left England, Shelley saw her cliffs for the last time. Previous to this, he had spent some time with Byron on Lac Léman, listening with admiration to stanzas of *Childe Harold* and indulging in outbursts of Rousseauism, as he rowed past the scenes associated with that philosopher. Now, his destination was Este where he would be i. proximity to Byron, then living in state at Venice. It is Byron who figures as the Count in *Julian and Maddalo*—a wonderful experiment in autobiography, lit with a rapturous enthusiasm for the new-found scenery :

> How beautiful is sunset, when the glow
> Of heaven descends upon a land like thee,
> Thou paradise of exiles—Italy.

A lost drama of Æschylus supplied the central idea of Shelley's *Prometheus Unbound*, but the scheme belongs to a later age. Essentially a lyrical drama, the spirit of Liberty, personified in Prometheus, constitutes the centre of the action. But the fauns and furies, spirits and echoes, that people the atmosphere of the new play, have no counterpart in Greek, and belong, rather, to the tradition of the *Midsummer Night's Dream.* As for Prometheus himself, he represents the spirit of revolt, tempered by Shelley's intense love for humanity :

> I would fain
> Be what it is my destiny to be,
> The saviour and the strength of suffering man.

It is Asia who voices Shelley's claim for his personification of Liberty and Love in Prometheus, and with the ideal of a restored humanity the drama comes to a close.

In the *Cenci,* on the other hand, a product of

Shelley's Italian studies, poetic qualities are brought into subjection to stage requirements, and the play ranks high among modern tragedies. Beatrice falls in consequence of her method of righting her wrongs—a method opposed to the moral order, though she is prevented from realizing this owing to a defect which constitutes the tragic ἁμαρτία in the Aristotelian sense. Like *Prometheus*, the *Cenci* is a challenge, though more closely related to actuality. The influence of Schiller's *Robbers*, which is specially prominent, serves to remind us of the extent of current German influence.

Adonais (1821), considered by some the greatest elegy in English, by others second only to *Lycidas*, is Shelley's lament for Keats whom he had apparently met in 1817. The two became so far familiar as to arrange for the production of rival poems, to be completed in six months. Shelley was first in the field with *Laon and Cythna*, followed after the prescribed limit by *Endymion*. Shelley was impressed by the wealth of imagination in Keats's poem, but thought it marked by " indistinct profusion." Keats's health showed signs of breakdown early in 1820, and, though Shelley invited him to Pisa, they did not meet again. Keats died at Rome in February, 1821, and about May Shelley began the composition of *Adonais*. The Hellenistic furore led him to a Greek model, and, in the lament of Moschus for Bion, a classic precedent lay to hand. For further suggestions, Shelley was indebted to Bion's *Elegy on Adonais*, which he had already partially translated into blank verse.

In its English form this exquisitely conceived lament for a brother poet is saturated with the spirit of poetry, and pulsates with sensations of a spirit world. A slight portrait of Shelley lies embedded in its stanzas—a portrait of that " frail form, a phantom among men," who " had gazed on Nature's naked loveliness, Actæon-like," and " fled astray with feeble steps o'er the world's wilderness." It is the outpouring of a spirit, whose being had felt life's pangs, whose sweetest songs had told of saddest thoughts, and who now longed to follow Adonais "beyond the shadow of our night." The personal element bulks no larger in *Adonais* than in *Lycidas*, but this Shelley replaces by his sense of kinship with the poet and lover of beauty. In construction, *Adonais* closely resembles *Lycidas*. It falls into three parts—the first expressing the poet's sense of loss for one who has been cut off ere his prime. The second contains the symbolic lamentation of Urania and the shepherds, combined with a denunciation of those, to whom Shelley attributed Keats's death, while the third is a call to rapture, for Keats is not dead but made one with Nature. The greatest passages in *Adonais* derive neither from Bion nor Moschus, for Shelley's thoughts turned rather towards that Infinite essence, into which he conceived Keats to be absorbed, and the poem concludes on a note of triumph. The pastoral element plays a slighter part in *Adonais* than in *Lycidas*, and only for a brief interval does Keats appear as a shepherd mourned by shepherds. Yet the elegy is permeated by that idealization of Beauty, Liberty, and Love, characteristic of Shelley's work.

Exquisite songs lie embedded in Shelley's dramas, like pearls set in a chaplet. Other and more independent compositions, permeated by the spirit of nature and born under an Italian sun, stand foremost in the English anthology. The *Cloud*, the *Skylark*, and the *Ode to the West Wind*, perhaps the most marvellous mystical poem in literature, are only the best known of these. The opening songs in *Hellas* anticipate Tennyson's dream-melodies; there is even greater achievement in the verses to *Constantia*, the *Lament*, and *When the Lamp is Shattered*:

> When hearts have once mingled
> Love first leaves the well-built nest;
> The weak one is singled
> To endure what it once possessed.

> O Love! who bewailest
> The frailty of all things here,
> Why choose you the frailest
> For your cradle, your home, and your bier?

By such songs Shelley has earned for himself a place among the greatest lyric poets in our literature. He has often been regarded as lacking in humour, but there are *Swellfoot the Tyrant*, *Peter Bell the Third*, the *Cyclops*, and the *Hymn to Mercury* to disprove this. His best known work reveals him as an artist, first and foremost. In 1815 he had pronounced Lucan's *Pharsalia* " of wonderful genius and transcending Virgil," but in the *Ode to Naples* his thoughts turned first to Homer and Virgil. Even *Queen Mab* came under his revising hand, and, of its nine cantos, all but portions of four were rejected. The impression of unreality derived from much of his work is due partly to his choice of similes. For he is essentially the poet of the clouds, the glaciers, and the sunrise, and the scenery described is largely unfamiliar. Perhaps the *Skylark* illustrates most effectively his method of progressing by a series of symbols, which, though they do not tend to the concrete, are admirably adapted for the end in view. Though Matthew Arnold described Shelley as a " beautiful and ineffectual angel," he faced problems as an artist, realizing that the greatest of problems is life itself. If a poet give us nothing beyond his " fair, unsought discoveries by the way," he has achieved much, yet Shelley has done more, for the sudden and inexplicable glories upon which he lights speak of truth beyond, even though this elude the questing imagination :

> On an unimagined shore,
> Under the grey beak of some promontory,
> She met me, robed in such exceeding glory,
> That I beheld her not.
>
> —*Epipsychidion*.

XIII

LAMB

CHARLES LAMB has been described as at once the sweetest, sanest, and most humane of English prose writers. His genius developed on novel lines, and he is equally significant in the departments of the essay and of criticism. Lamb may be regarded from several points of view. He was a new writer with a unique style, representing a definite reaction against eighteenth century ideals; and, at the same time, a literary discoverer who did much to resuscitate the Elizabethans. His *Essays* are invaluable as self-revelations, and as impressions of contemporaries.

The record of Lamb's life is to be found scattered throughout his prose and letters—the facts have been arranged and commented upon in the biographies of Ainger and Lucas.

In the essay on the *Old Benchers of the Inner Temple* Lamb gave his early impressions of his father and his father's employer, Samuel Salt. Ties of the closest affection bound Charles to his sister Mary, whom he has celebrated as Bridget Elia in the essay entitled *Mackery End*. The pair seem to have availed themselves of old Samuel Salt's library, the scene of Charles's "kindly engendure," and there, no doubt, he read for the first time such books as the *Complete Angler* and *Pilgrim's Progress*. The essay, *My Relations*, makes it probable that Lamb owed a good deal to the sobering influence of his maiden aunt, Sarah Lamb, of whom he speaks in the story of Mary Howe, in the series entitled *Mrs. Leicester's School*: "The attention and fondness which she showed to me, conscious as I was that I was almost the only being she felt anything like fondness to, made me love her, as it was natural; indeed, I am ashamed to say that I fear I almost loved her better than both my parents put together. But there was an oddness, a silence about my aunt, which was never interrupted but by her occasional expressions of love to me, that made me stand in fear of her." The essay is additionally valuable for the glimpses it affords of Lamb's reading. He made out enough of the *Book of Martyrs* to fill his head with vanity : " I used to think I was so courageous I could be burnt too, and would put my hands upon the flames which were pictured in the pretty pictures which the book had and feel them." There was, besides, Culpepper's *Herbal*, " full of pictures of plants and herbs," though he did not much care for this, and the illustration in Stackhouse's *History of the Bible* of the Ark and the beasts getting into it, which gave him particular delight, even though it puzzled him. Lastly, there was Glanville's *Considerations touching Witches and Witchcraft*, a well-thumbed volume, with the strangest of strange stories.

During this period Lamb paid visits to his grand-mother, Mary Field, at Blakesware, and to her sister, Mrs. Gladman, at Mackery End. The record of impressions may be found in the essays, entitled *Mackery End*, *Blakesmoor in H—shire*, *Dream Children*, and the *Last Peach*, besides the *Gem* for 1830, in which he describes his grandmother :

But of all her nostrums—rest her soul—nothing came up to the Saturday Night's Flannel—that rude fragment of a Witney blanket—Wales spins none so coarse—thrust into the corners of a weak child's eye with soap that might have absterged an Ethiop, whitened the hands of Duncan's She-murderer, and scoured away Original Sin itself.

It was at Mr. William Bird's day-school in a court off Fetter Lane that Charles and Mary Lamb received their

early schooling, but at the age of seven Charles passed
on to the Blue Coat School, Christ's Hospital, where
he remained for seven years. Writing in 1825, Lamb
recalls his impressions of Mr. Bird's school : " O, how
I remember our legs wedged into those uncomfortable
sloping desks, where we sat elbowing each other—and
the injunctions to attain a free hand, unattainable in
that position; the first copy I wrote after, with its moral
lesson, ' Art improves Nature '; the still earlier pot-
hooks and the hangers, some traces of which I fear may
yet be apparent in this manuscript; the truant looks
sidelong to the garden, which seemed a mockery to our
imprisonment; the prize for best spelling, which had
almost turned my head, and which to this day I cannot
reflect upon without a vanity, which I ought to be
ashamed of; our little leaden inkstands, not separately
subsisting, but sunk into the desks; the bright,
punctually-washed morning fingers, darkening gradually
with another and another ink-spot : what a world of
little associated circumstances, pains and pleasures
mingling their quotas of pleasure, arise at the reading
of those few simple words—' Mr. William Bird, an
eminent Writer, and Teacher of languages and
mathematics in Fetter Lane, Holborn."

Lamb's impressions of Christ's Hospital are set forth
in the essays of 1813 and 1820. Among the new boys
was Samuel Taylor Coleridge, who gives his own
impressions of the school in the *Biographia Literaria* :
Coleridge's influence over Lamb was destined to be
continuous. At Christ's Hospital Lamb acquired
proficiency in Latin, but never passed beyond the
deputy-Grecians, the select circle of the Grecians proper
being restricted to those intending to proceed to the
Universities. Lamb left Christ's Hospital in 1789,
and, after an interval of two years, entered the South
Sea House. Though his sojourn there was brief, the
impressions imbibed were vivid, and form a prominent
element in the *Elia* essays of 1823. In 1792 he was

appointed clerk in the accountant's office of the India House, an institution with which he maintained connexion during the next thirty years. The death in that year of Samuel Salt involved the Lamb family in difficulties; they were forced to leave the Inner Temple, and to make the best they could of their means. At the close of 1794 we are afforded a glimpse of Lamb in company with Coleridge at the Salutation Tavern, Newgate Street. It is probable that Lamb's emotions had already been stirred by a visit to Blakesware, during which he first set eyes on the Alice W—— of the *Blakesmoor* essay. Coleridge was in similar case, and, at the moment, the two friends must have been unusually communicative. The romance of Lamb's early life was, however, to experience a severe shock. His relations with Alice W—— ended in the course of a year or two, and the tragic death of his mother by his sister's hand involved the rest of his life in gloom. Mary Lamb, like Charles himself, was prone to fits of insanity, and, after the tragedy of September, 1796, she remained under the guardianship of her brother for the rest of his life.

Lamb's correspondence—an invaluable source of information with respect to his life—begins with a letter to Coleridge, dated May 27th, 1769, in which he refers jestingly to his "confinement." In a letter of September 27th he describes the tragic events of the preceding day. Henceforth, he was wedded to the fortunes of his sister and his father, though the latter survived only till 1799.

At this period Lamb's literary instincts found an outlet in verse. The sonnets of 1795 speak, in part, of blighted affections, and have reference to his relations with Alice W——: other verses are addressed to his sister and to Charles Lloyd. In 1798 Lamb contributed to the volume of *Blank Verse*, of which he was joint-author along with Charles Lloyd, the most remarkable of his poems, the tender piece entitled the *Old Familiar Faces*. *Rosamund Gray*, Lamb's first prose venture, appeared in the same year, and its idyllic charm drew forth the commendation of Shelley. Like its model, the *Julia de Roubigné* of Mackenzie, it took the form of letters. But Lamb had no constructive gifts and, despite the passing interest attaching to Rosamund, no doubt a resuscitation of Alice W——, the story fails to convince.

Coleridge left for Germany at the close of 1798, but, before this, he and Lamb had fallen out, Lamb's last letter making the rupture inevitable.

From 1801-1804 Lamb made efforts to increase his scanty income by contributing jokes and dramatic criticisms to the *Morning Post*, the *Morning Chronicle*, and the *Albion*. The best comment on these jocularities is Lamb's own : " Somebody has said that to swallow six cross-buns daily consecutively for a fortnight would surfeit the stoutest digestion. But to have to furnish as many jokes daily, and that not for a fortnight, but for a long twelvemonth, as we are constrained to do, was a little harder execution." Yet the following comment on Locke's doctrine of the sheet of white paper is surely excellent : " It must be confessed that whoever wrote upon Locke's mind has left large margins," and there were others equal to it.

Lamb's first play, *John Woodvil* (1802), was somewhat severely handled by the critics of the *Edinburgh Review* and the *Annual Register*. It proved too archaic for Lamb's contemporaries, and was, dramatically, ill-calculated to hold an audience. As literature, it may, however, be estimated differently. It was a successful attempt by an ardent student of our older drama to write an original play in the spirit of the Elizabethans, an Arcadian romance with the breath of the dawn upon it. Its *raison d'être* is explained by Lamb himself : " When I first wrote *John Woodvil*, Beaumont and Fletcher and Massinger were then a first love, and what wonder if my language imperceptibly took a tinge," and *John Woodvil* remains the earliest of modern efforts to revive the atmosphere of Elizabethan drama. *Mr. H.*, Lamb's second play, ran for two nights at Drury Lane. The point of the farce lay in the sensational downfall of the hero, consequent upon the disclosure of his name, and in the clever device whereby he was re-instated. Unfortunately, the names, Hogsflesh and Bacon, were familiar to the audience, and, when the climax came, interest vanished. The report in *Monthly Literary Recreations* runs: "The audience were disgusted, and the farce went on to its very conclusion almost unheard, amidst the contending clamours of 'Silence,' 'Hear, hear!' and 'Off, off, off!'" It is stated, however, that *Mr. H* ran with extraordinary success at Philadelphia during the year 1812.

Lamb's first successful venture belongs to 1807. Some two years earlier he had met Hazlitt, and was introduced by him to Godwin. At this moment, Godwin was setting up a publishing firm for the production of children's books, and a trifle of Lamb's, the *King and Queen of Hearts* (1805), was issued in a series priced 1s. plain and 1s. 6d. coloured. The production of children's books continued to interest him and, in conjunction with his sister Mary, he published in 1807 his chief contribution to this class of literature and his first successful venture. The *Tales from Shakespeare*, a series of prose versions of twenty Shakespearian plays, were mainly the work of Mary Lamb, Charles being responsible merely for the *Tragedies*. Lamb claimed to be answerable for "occasionally a tale piece or correction of grammar, for none of the cuts (a hit at the illustrator Mulready) and all of the spelling." "The rest," he goes on, "is my sister's. We think *Pericles* of hers the best, and *Othello* of mine, but I hope all have some good. *As You Like It* we like least. So much, only begging you to tear out the cuts and give them to Johnny, as 'Mrs. Godwin's fancy.'" The *Tales from Shakespeare* form an admirable condensation of their originals, with a happy blend of quotation and a characteristic sympathy with the child-mind. Immensely popular in England, they have been translated into French, German, and other languages. Lamb continued to produce books for children for some years, the *Adventures of Ulysses* (1808), *Mrs. Leicester's School* (1809), *Poetry for Children* (1809), and *Prince Dorus* (1811).

English romantic criticism was largely influenced by Schlegel and Lessing, but it would be a mistake in view of the eighteenth century work of Pope, Theobald, Warburton, Johnson, and Malone, to assume that appreciation of Shakespeare came to England from abroad. Among English critics, precedence is probably due to Coleridge, who was followed rapidly by Lamb with his *Tales from Shakespeare* and *Specimens of Elizabethan Dramatists* (1808). The notes on Coleridge's lectures were not published till 1817, and in that year appeared Hazlitt's *Characters of Shakespeare's Plays*. In his autobiography, Lamb modestly claims to have been " the first to draw the public attention to the old English dramatists in a work called *Specimens of English Dramatic Writers who lived about the time of Shakespeare*, published about fifteen years ago." This claim posterity has fully recognized. The study of Elizabethan drama had occupied Lamb for at least a dozen years before he produced his *Specimens*. He had filled his notebooks with extracts suitable for such a volume, drawing upon the stalls of second-hand shops and the shelves of the British Museum. The selection was generally admirable, and the notes proved him the critic born, for whom Heywood's sweet domesticity had no less attraction than the fire of Tourneur or the daring of Webster. " The world has need," as Swinburne put it, " to give thanks to so great and so generous a benefactor; who has fed us on lion's marrow, and with honey out of the lion's mouth. To him and to him alone it is that we owe the revelation and the resurrection of our greatest dramatic poets after Shakespeare."

Lamb gave further indications of critical ability in his *Hogarth* and the *Tragedies of Shakespeare*, published in Leigh Hunt's *Reflector* in 1811, and during the same period he produced important essays, *Recollections of Christ's Hospital* (1813) and *Confessions of a Drunkard* (1814). His *Works*, as far as completed, were issued in a two-volume edition in 1818.

But the *Essays of Elia* were yet to come—published in two series, as *Elia* (1823) and *Last Essays of Elia* (1833). Lamb explains that the name Elia (properly Ellia) was derived from an Italian clerk at the South Sea House. With half a dozen exceptions, the whole of the essays had appeared previously in the *London Magazine*, with which were associated at different dates De Quincey, Hood, Carlyle, and Landor.

The *Essays of Elia* represent the fine flower of Lamb's genius, and are, first and foremost, personal revelations. Whatever interpretation we put upon the old dictum of Buffon's that " Style is the man," it is certain that it can be applied literally to Lamb's writings. At every stage he reminds us of Montaigne, of the subjective rather than the objective method. In this type of essay a trace of egotism is inevitable, hence its autobiographic character. Lamb sought his models in older writers of the Elizabethan and Jacobean periods —in Sir Thomas Browne, Burton, and others. He himself has been called the last of the Elizabethans, but the attempt to revive the atmosphere of a bygone period sometimes produces an effect of over-elaboration. The subtle wit and often freakish imagination, couched in an eclectic and allusive diction, demand an ear attuned. Instance the following from the *Old and the New Schoolmaster*:

" Rest to the souls of those fine old Pedagogues; the breed, long since extinct, of the Lilys, and the Linacres : who, believing that all learning was contained in the languages which they taught, and despising every other acquirement as superficial and useless, came to their task as to a sport! Revolving in a perpetual cycle of declensions, conjugations, syntaxes, and prosodies; renewing constantly the occupations which had charmed their studious childhood; rehearsing continually the part of the past; life must have slipped from them at last like one day. They were always in their first garden, reaping harvests of their golden time, among their *Flori* and their *Spici-legia*; in Arcadia still, but kings; the ferule of their sway not much harsher, but of like dignity with that mild sceptre attributed to King Basileus; the Greek and Latin, their stately Pamela and their Philoclea; with the occasional duncery of some untoward tyro, serving for a refreshing interlude of a Mopsa or a clown Damœtas! "

Yet it was Lamb's boast that he would write for posterity, and this he has fully justified. Their sanity, fanciful delicacy, and imaginative sympathy, combined with an all-pervading humour, impart to the *Elia* essays their unique attraction. Altogether averse from mysticism, Lamb loved human faces and the traces of human activity in town or city. For the quiet of green fields he had a tender affection, but no such reverence as could alienate him from the busy haunts of men. Asked for an account of his impressions of Cumberland, he replied he was obliged to think of the ham and beef shop near St. Martin's Lane in order to bring his thoughts from their painful elevation to the sober regions of everyday life.

Lamb is revealed to us, first and foremost, in his *Essays* and *Letters,* but there are other sources of information as to his character and appearance in the impressions of Proctor, Haydon, Talfourd, Crabb Robinson, De Quincey, and Hazlitt. As described by himself, his appearance was " a compound of the Jew, the gentleman, and the angel." His love of nonsense, his jokes, his characteristic and sometimes intentional stutter were noted by one or other observer, and stories survive to illustrate his convivial and agreeable relations with his friends.

" Oh! for the pen of John Buncle to consecrate a *petit souvenir* to their memory! There was L[amb] himself, the most delightful, the most provoking, the most witty and sensible of men. He always made the best pun, and the best remark in the course of the evening. His serious conversation, like his serious writing, is his best. No one ever stammered out such fine, piquant, deep, eloquent things in half a dozen half sentences as he does. His jests scald like tears: and he probes a question with a play upon words. What a keen, laughing, hair-brained vein of home-felt truth! What choice venom! How often did we cut into the haunch of letters, while we discussed the haunch of mutton on the table! How we skimmed the cream of criticism! How we got into the heart of controversy! How we picked out the marrow of authors! ' And, in our flowing cups, many a good name and true was freshly remembered.' " (Hazlitt : *On the Conversation of Authors*.)

XIV

GREAT VICTORIANS

I. CARLYLE AND MACAULAY

THE year 1830 forms a fairly clear landmark in the history of nineteenth century literature. It marks pretty accurately the close of the Revolutionary epoch and the opening of the interregnum. In or about that year the great figures of the preceding period left the stage. Byron died in 1824, Goethe and Scott in 1832, Coleridge and Lamb in 1834; but Southey lingered till 1843, and Wordsworth, curiously enough, till 1850, the year of *Pendennis* and *Copperfield*, of *In Memoriam* and the *Christmas Eve*. From 1830 to 1840 the literary arena was occupied by a crowd of minor poets—Mrs. Hemans, Hood, Praed, and Motherwell. Tennyson and Browning were, as yet, labouring in obscurity, Carlyle and Dickens alone among men of note obtaining general recognition. The year 1840, on the other hand, marks the close of the transition period and the beginning of the Victorian age proper. By 1842 Tennyson had acquired a right to the dictatorship, and, henceforward, dominates the world of letters till well-nigh the close of the century. Indeed, Tennyson, Browning, and Elizabeth Barrett were for the Victorian period what Wordsworth, Coleridge, and Southey had been for the Revolutionary. By 1840, however, revolutionary feeling had ceased to shake England, the middle classes had succeeded in asserting a position, and, henceforth, play an active and comparatively orderly part in politics. The peculiar problems of the age arose out of the new political and economic conditions, and, though the doctrines of human perfectibility and of a return to nature had ceased to inflame men's minds, authors were forced to grapple with the newer problems arising out of the existence of a great democracy.

Between the Revolutionary and the Victorian epochs there were further points of difference arising out of changed atmospheric conditions. The poetry of the earlier period, kindled though it was by boundless enthusiasm, had been apt to rely upon this at the expense of intellect. Shelley is a case in point, if we recall the extent to which his work was based on Godwinian formulæ. A wider culture, combined with a decreased interest in formulæ, is apparent later. Yet the kinship of the two schools is obvious. Speculation is still rampant in the agitation of the closing nineteenth century, and self-consciousness permeates its poetry, however differently this may express itself in Browning as compared with Shelley. The outlook of the new age was influenced by other factors—the great Peace Exhibition at the Crystal Palace in 1851 and the Darwinian hypothesis of 1859. These "challenges from man to man" compelled attention to the facts of history, with a consequent endeavour to express them in literature. As regards method, there was a close "organic" connexion between the Tennysonian and the Wordsworthian schools. Romanticism continued in vogue, but the pressure of nineteenth century thought threatened, at times, an over-intellectualized poetry. In prose, the scientific movement of the century, with the consequent modification of theological conceptions, was largely responsible for the Victorian school, represented by Carlyle, Ruskin, Newman, and Macaulay. In dealing with individual writers Carlyle and Macaulay may be selected as representative historians and essayists, Dickens and Thackeray as writers of fiction.

Carlyle may be regarded from several points of view; he was, at one and the same time, critic, historian, and satirist. But any discussion of his position as man of letters brings one face to face with the problem of his style. The literary method, dubbed Carlylese, was matured in the seclusion of Craigenputtock, the early *Life of Schiller* being free from mannerisms, instance the following passage :

" Among those (then at Weimar) the chief in all respects was Goethe. It was during his present visit that Schiller first met with this illustrious person; concerning whom, both by reading and report, his expectations had been raised so high. No two men, both of exalted genius, could be possessed of more different sorts of excellence, than the two that were now brought together, in a large company of their mutual friends."

Of Carlyle's later and characteristic manner much has been set down to German influence, to Richter, in particular, instance his non-English syntactical arrangement and foreign idiom. Other stylistic tricks—exclamations, apostrophes, abrupt transitions, omission of particles, and neologisms—he possibly owed to his Scottish ancestry. Sir Thomas Urquhart, the translator of Rabelais, was his equal in respect of word-coinage and slang, and wielded as prodigious a vocabulary. Johnson, too, shows a trace of Carlylese. But to consider Carlyle's style exclusively on its technical side is to miss half its inspiration. The style is the man, and the denunciatory, ethical, and humorous expression of *Sartor Resartus* is but a revelation of its author's personality. Carlyle's prose may be parodied, but it eludes imitation. Of late it has fallen into some disrepute, yet, apart from verbal tricks, will assuredly live among the greatest of inspirations.

Though Carlyle's critical work is, by no means, equal, it was, as a whole, little less than epoch-making. He was among the first to supply the English public with an adequate account of German literature—a field in which Coleridge and De Quincey had preceded him. He has appreciations of the *Nibelungen Lied*, of Heine, Richter, Novalis, Schiller, and Goethe, justifying the latter's remark that he " is more at home in our literature than we are ourselves." In his *Life of Schiller* he supplied, along with his own rendering of particular passages, detailed appreciations of each of the German plays. As for Goethe, he regarded him less as a poet and scientist than as a spiritual force. Of his English essays those on Burns and Scott are the most noteworthy; Carlyle probes to the heart of Burns and is tolerant of his failings. Sceptical regarding the value of the untrained democrat, he recognized to the full the worth of the individual, and Burns remained for him the typical peasant, a product of Scottish national life. " Impelled by the expansive movement of his own irrepressible soul, he struggles forward into the general view; and with haughty modesty lays down before us, as the fruit of his labour, a gift, which Time has now pronounced imperishable." With Scott, on the other hand, he had less sympathy. He denied him greatness, and, while admitting the importance of the *Waverley* series, held that he failed to create living characters, fashioning them, rather, from the skin inwards. Unfortunately, a prejudice in favour of what he deemed the serious side of literature blinded Carlyle to the merits of Keats and Shelley, Lamb and Coleridge, and much of his criticism remains distinctly ethical.

As an historian Carlyle ranks among the greatest. Possessed of unabated energy, he spared no labour in the acquisition of detail, and in the *French Revolution* surpassed the Germans in their own field. With a passion for the concrete, rather than the abstract, side of history, Carlyle dealt less with principles than with individual scenes and characters. The *French Revolution* thus became a portrait gallery and a study in episode : an " essence of innumerable biographies." Scientific history it hardly claims to be, nor are its parts equal. The French Revolution neither began with the taking of the Bastille, nor ended with the triumph of Napoleon. But, despite omissions and inaccuracies, the work towers above most so-called scientific history, and its imaginative grasp sets it outside the range of the average historian. Conceiving history as a study of the relationship of man to the universe, Carlyle concerned himself, as Goethe and Fichte had done, with the eternal struggle between belief and unbelief. Cromwell, as known to us to-day, was his discovery, yet the *Life* proved less a work of art than a monument of research. It survives as the noblest of tributes to one whose character has been infected by the calumnies of centuries, and whose merits have been suffered to lapse into oblivion. The *Life of Frederick the Great*, again, reveals monumental industry, though industry somewhat misdirected, for here the historian laboured under difficulties, and his enthusiasm was hardly maintained to the end. The book is overloaded with detail, and the central figure tends to be merged in the crowd.

Carlyle made his appearance in literature as a revolutionary force. He throbs with a spirit of denunciation of false creeds, false morals, and false politics. He belonged to no political party; his early enthusiasm for democracy suffered eclipse, and earth remained to him "one fuliginous dust-heap." Hence his doctrine of the superman or Übermensch, in which again he expands Fichte. The Teufelsdröckh of *Sartor* is conceived in his own image, and, like his creator, dwells apart from men. *Sartor Resartus* thus provides a summary of Carlyle's philosophy, and the history of his escape from materialism represented by the Everlasting No to the outlook of spiritual freedom represented by the Everlasting Yea : " Here in this poor, miserable, hampered, despicable Actual, wherein thou even now standest, here or nowhere is thy Ideal; work it out therefore, and working, believe, live, be free." There is further the idea of *Entsagen*, Renunciation, Liberation from external things, which he owed to

Goethe. Doubtless, Carlyle's mind was gradually soured by lack of recognition : he was an apostle of a new creed with a contempt for a newer. " The *Origin of Species*," he writes, " showed up the capricious stupidity of mankind; never could read a page of it and waste the least thought upon it." Yet his own gospel has permeated the thought of later generations, and suffers, if anything, from over-familiarity. Its insistence on primal duties has begun to weary a generation, for whom both Carlyle's Puritanism and Goethe's *Ehrfurcht* have lost much of their significance.

To his political doctrines the present age is, likewise, antipathetic, for, while Carlyle recognized no aristocracy save that of character and intellect, he was equally denunciatory of democracy. For the collective intelligence he had no respect, denouncing its shibboleths, ballot-boxes, " dog-hood suffrage," and " froth-logic," while Right ever remained to him the " eternal symbol of Might."

Excluding the novelists, no prose writer of the early part of the nineteenth century was more popular in his day than Macaulay, nor has anyone maintained a more persistent influence. Despite the fact that his method has been regarded with hostility, his influence over the general reader remains paramount. Macaulay interests by his many-sidedness. He was, at one and the same time, poet, politician, historian, biographer, and essayist, with an unquestioned reputation as an orator. At the same time, he has endeared himself by his private virtues, and, in the pages of Trevelyan's biography, is depicted as consistently amiable, sincere, and honourable. With children " he was the best of playfellows, unrivalled in the invention of games and never weary of repeating them." He was tenacious in friendship, clinging to those he had long known, but averse from new attachments. Macaulay attracts by his optimism— the optimism of one who found himself famous at twenty-five. In this respect he proved the antithesis of Carlyle whose outlook upon life was consistently morose. The political and literary sides of Macaulay's career were interconnected. He wrote his *Essay on Milton* at the age of twenty-five, while still seeking a career, but, from 1830 to 1847, was actively associated with politics, and the politician is reflected in the man-of-letters. Macaulay's speeches are characterized by the lucidity and persuasive power observable in the *Essays*. Lacking the lofty eloquence of Burke, they yet held the House by their sonorous vocabulary and apt illustration. Macaulay's parliamentary career was broken by a four years' sojourn in India (1834-8), but during the last twelve years of his life his energies were almost exclusively devoted to literature.

Of Macaulay's verse little need be said. It has much in common with that of Scott and the balladists, rapidity of movement, vivid outline, and enthusiasm. Macaulay commanded a vigorous narrative, best exemplified in the *Lays of Ancient Rome* (1843):

> Alone stood brave Horatius
>   But constant still in mind;
> Thrice thirty thousand foes before
>   And the broad flood behind.
> " Down with him," cried false Sextus,
>   With a smile on his pale face.
> " Now yield thee," cried Lars Porsena,
>   " Now yield thee to our grace."

We seek here in vain for the highest qualities, though verse of this nature, informed with life and energy, constitutes no mean contribution to literature. In the ballad on the *Battle of Naseby*, however, Macaulay struck a deeper note, and the opening stanzas ring with that deepest of human passions—religious hatred :

> Oh! wherefore come ye forth, in triumph from the North,
>   With your hands and your feet and your raiment all red?
> And wherefore doth your rout send forth a joyous shout?
>   And whence be the grapes of the wine-press which ye tread?
>
> Oh evil was the root, and bitter was the fruit,
>   And crimson was the juice of the vintage that we trod;

For we trampled on the throng of the haughty and the strong
Who sate in the high places and slew the saints of God.

As an essayist, Macaulay's popularity remains
unrivalled. The *Essays* were published in 1843 in
volume form, and, though ostensibly reviews, each is in
reality an independent piece, for which the book under
consideration serves merely as a peg. The enormous
success of the collection was due to the author's gift of
popularization and to his style. A typical Whig of
the Reform period, Macaulay shared with the average
Englishman his contempt for ideas and aversion for
romance. A profound believer in the value of common
sense, he distrusted anything that failed to appeal to
the evidence of the senses. His style reflects these
qualities, and makes an immediate appeal by its per-
spicuity, its illustration, and its emphasis. Macaulay
has no obscurities; one may question, but cannot
mistake the author's point of view. He has popularized
history and literature to such a degree that many have
derived their ideas in these departments exclusively from
the *Essays*. Nor can his influence in promoting the
methods of later journalese be overestimated. These
characteristics, excellent in many respects, aroused
hostility in critical circles, and Carlyle, in his intense
fashion, labelled Macaulay " a poor creature, with his
dictionary literature and his saloon arrogance . . . no
vision in him . . . will neither see nor do anything
great." But this is the old antagonism between the
popular peer and the morose sage. Matthew Arnold,
for whom Macaulay represented the incarnation of
Philistinism, was largely responsible for the reaction
against his popularity. He insisted " that much of
Macaulay's excellence lies on the surface," and that
his very perspicuity may be an illusion. For example,
Frederic Harrison pointed out how, in the essay on
the *History of the Popes*, Macaulay insists upon the
permanent elements in the Papacy, drawing upon his
vast stores of learning to embroider his theme. We

gaze back to the days when " the smoke of sacrifice rose from the Pantheon," forward into the dim period " when some traveller from New Zealand shall, in the midst of a vast solitude, take his stand on a broken arch of London Bridge to sketch the ruins of St. Paul's." Provided we do not pause to consider that the Papacy is not identical with the Catholic Church, and that its actual duration has been surpassed by that of other institutions, we are carried away by the orator. But reflection dispels the dream, and the discovery of the writer's insincerity repels us. Again, his emphasis is often marred by prejudice—the prejudice of the anti-monarchical Whig. The crimes of the Stuarts were glaring enough, but Macaulay has deprived them of the last vestiges of humanity : " The race, accursed of God and man, was a second time driven forth, to wander on the face of the earth, and to be a byword and a shaking of the head to the nations." Much may be conceded to genuine indignation, but, when a writer appears to be striving after pure effect, one is apt to be repelled by his over-emphasis. There is a difference between the identification of Charles and James with Belial and Moloch and the suggestion that Boswell is immortal *because* he was " a dunce, a parasite, and a coxcomb." In the former case, the intensity arises from genuine emotion ; in the latter, we are face to face with a paradox. Macaulay's literary method partook largely of the nature of public oratory; his style was essentially rhetorical. His repetitions, his antitheses, his paragraphs were alike designed to persuade. He was not eclectic, nor had he any power of subtle suggestion, yet his effects depend upon the most careful elaboration. His manner is to alternate the short and long sentence, combining them into a prose paragraph. He had, besides, an apt command of detail, for which he drew upon vast stores of memory. A writer who, as report has it, could have rewritten *Paradise Lost* had every copy been lost, may be pardoned for assuming that his reader has the wide acquaintance with literature and history ascribed to his famous schoolboy. Thus, " Every schoolboy knows who imprisoned Montezuma, and who strangled Atahualpa," or again, " Every schoolgirl knows the lines,

> Scarce had lamented Forbes paid
> The tribute to his Minstrel's shade.

Macaulay delighted in antithetical effects :

> He had a head which statuaries loved to copy, and a foot the deformity of which the beggars in the streets mimicked.—*Byron*.

But his emphasis was constantly misdirected. There is exaggeration in the *Essay on Johnson*, still more in that on Madame D'Arblay : " Had she been a negro slave, a humane planter would have excused her from work : but Her Majesty showed no mercy." Indeed, the Queen degenerates into an Old Fury, and Madame Schwellenberg into a hateful toad-eater. As for his criticism, this suffers by reason of its limitations. Macaulay confessed to liking no books or people, to whom he had not been accustomed from boyhood, and had no taste for romantic literature, though entirely in sympathy with the eighteenth century. In matters of abstract literary theory he sometimes went astray. " Poetry," he informs us, " produces an illusion on the eye of the mind, as a magic lantern produces an illusion on the eye of the body. And, as the magic lantern acts best in a dark room, poetry effects its purpose most completely in a dark age. . . . We cannot unite the incompatible advantages of reality and deception, the clear discernment of truth and the exquisite enjoyment of fiction." There is a degree of truth in his remarks on the heroic couplet as practised by Addison and Pope, but that " the art is as mechanical as that of mending a kettle or shoeing a horse " may well be denied. His happiest efforts are to be found in the *Essay on the Comic Dramatists of the Restoration* and in the short biographies of Goldsmith and Johnson, contributed to the *Encyclopædia Britannica*.

Macaulay's *History of England* ranks second in popularity only to his *Essays*. It narrates the events of 1685-1701 in such detail that, on the same scale, " the history of England from Alfred would," according to Frederic Harrison, " require five hundred similar volumes." But Macaulay has mastered his materials, and imparts to the dry facts of history the interest of a novel. He excels in presenting a lively panorama of events, and plans his whole with unique skill. But the speculative side of history was to him an unexplored region; and in his attention to facts he tended to ignore principles. A philosophical historian Macaulay never was; he is essentially an historical portrait-painter.

II. DICKENS AND THACKERAY

The fame of Dickens has of late years suffered some eclipse, the natural penalty for his undisputed pre-eminence among his own generation. His England has largely disappeared : children no longer work thirteen hours a day in mines and factories, the gallows ceases to disfigure our public places, and excessive drinking has become a thing of the past. The Industrial Revolution swept away the stage-coach and created an order of things, of which Dickens's pages reflect the mere beginnings. Dickens's types are less familiar to the present generation, and, though not non-existent, must be sought in the remoter parts of our cities. His pathos offends a more sophisticated age, his humour is stigmatized as vulgar. Yet he has never lacked readers, and the permanent elements of his genius remain unchallenged.

The year 1834 is memorable as that in which Dickens's first sketch appeared, after having been " dropped stealthily one evening at twilight, with fear and trembling, into a dark letter-box, in a dark office, up a dark court in Fleet Street." This was afterwards printed in the *Sketches by Boz*, a series of stories contributed to the *Old Monthly Magazine* and the *Evening Chronicle* under the title of "Mr. Minns and his Cousin." These sketches contain all the elements of Dickens's later manner : minute observation, humour, and pathos. But the work is crude, the humour scarcely rising above farce, while the pathos tends to over-declamation. The faculty of observation is the most remarkable feature, and in this respect the *Sketches by Boz* constitute a literary phenomenon. Dickens, as he appeared at this time, has been described by Carlyle : "He is a fine little fellow—Boz, I think. Clear, blue, intelligent eyes, eyebrows that he arches amazingly, large protrusive rather loose mouth, which he shuttles about—eyebrows, eyes, mouth and all—in a very singular manner while speaking. Surmount this with a loose coil of common-coloured hair, and set it on a small compact figure, very small, and dressed à la D'Orsay rather than well—this is Pickwick. For the rest, a quiet, shrewd-looking little fellow, who seems to guess pretty well what he is and what others are." The dandified air here described is quite in accordance with what we should expect from the manners of the period.

The appearance of *Pickwick* in the early months of 1836 marks the beginning of the Victorian novel. Bulwer, Disraeli, and Marryat had already opened their careers, but Thackeray, George Eliot, and the Brontës were as yet unknown, and for years Dickens held the field without a rival. The genesis of *Pickwick* is a matter of peculiar literary interest. The letter-press was designed by the publishers to illustrate a series of sporting sketches drawn by the caricaturist Seymour. Dickens, however, was averse from the scheme, and insisted that the sketches should be subordinated to the narrative. The difficulty was overcome by Seymour's disastrous death soon after the appearance of the first number. *Pickwick* is essentially a picaresque novel of the type of *Don Quixote* or *Lazarillo de Tormes*. No design is apparent in the early chapters, and the story secured no immediate reputation. But, with the collapse of the original scheme, Dickens was able to follow his bent, and the appearance of Sam Weller in the fifth part raised the orders to 40,000. Episodic stories constitute a feature of the book which was planned on a large scale. The centres of interest lie in the characters rather than the story, though the minor figures seem farcical compared with Pickwick, that soul of geniality and good sense. This formlessness is largely to be accounted for by the method of publication, since a novelist writing on such a system must needs make each issue self-contained.

The experiment in comic epic succeeded so well that, before completing his first venture, Dickens started *Oliver Twist* in Bentley's *Miscellany* (1838). His artistic development is apparent in the plot of this second novel. Despite improbabilities, the story reveals a definite attempt at construction, though Dickens rarely succeeded in discovering plausible circumstances for his plots, and was apt to trust over much to coincidence, as, for instance, where Oliver runs up against his father's friend. Oliver, again, is a glaring improbability, and much of the dialogue is stagey. *Pickwick* had been in part an attack on existing debtors' prisons, *Oliver Twist* struck a blow at the idealized criminal, of whom Fielding's *Jonathan Wild* and Ainsworth's *Jack Sheppard* were outstanding examples. In Dickens's novel the haunts of London thieves doubtless owed much to his personal experiences of the city.

Nicholas Nickleby, begun in 1838 before the conclusion of *Oliver Twist*, is tragi-comedy, and the ugly character of the book, the usurer, Ralph Nickleby, proves less interesting than the comic figures, Mr. Crummles, Squeers, and Mrs. Mantalini. As a whole, *Nicholas Nickleby* betrays signs of having been written under pressure. As Dickens put it, " The conduct of three different stories at the same time, and the production of a large portion of each every month, would have been beyond Scott himself." Melodramatic situations abound towards the close which remains unconvincing.

The *Old Curiosity Shop* (1840-1) first appeared in the fourth number of *Master Humphrey's Clock*, a weekly periodical. The public had shown little interest in the essays and sketches contributed to the first three numbers, and a return to the novel-form seemed inevitable. The *Old Curiosity Shop*, with its idealized child-heroine, little Nell, Quilp, Dick Swiveller, and Sampson Brass, was the best novel so far written. It takes us into the open air and, in its enthusiasm for country life, steers clear of theatrical conventions. Dickens's prose frequently falls into blank verse, the result, Horne thought, " of harmonious accident," but a vice to which he was prone under the strain of emotion :

> Old men | were there
> Whose eyes | were dim | and sen | ses failing, || grandmothers
> Who might | have died | ten years | ago | and still
> Been old; || the deaf, | the blind, | the lame, | the palsied,
> The liv | ing dead | in ma | ny shapes | and forms,
> To see | the clos | ing of | that ear | ly grave.
> What was | the death | it would | shut in | to that
> Which still | could crawl | and creep | above it,

and again, in the description of Quilp's death :

> It toyed and sported with its ghastly freight,
> Now bruising it against the slimy piles,
> Now hiding it in mud or long rank grass.

With *Barnaby Rudge*, in part an historical novel concerned with the No Popery riots of 1780, and containing much ornate description, the first period of Dickens's career as a novelist came to a close. *Barnaby* has been praised for its construction. The chapters tend to open in an old-fashioned moralizing strain, and, altogether, it comes nearest to the manner of the *Tale of Two Cities*.

The American tour, on which Dickens started in January, 1842, widened his experiences, and served to make him conscious of the extent of his influence. He received " welcomes of all kinds, balls, dinners, assemblies without end. Deputations waited upon him from the cities, villages and towns, and even from the Far West." Public and private bodies showered honours upon him. It was not long, however, before Dickens's emotions changed. " There is no country on the face of the earth," he wrote, " where there is less freedom of opinion on any subject in reference to which there is a broad difference of opinion than in the United States." He had lectured the Americans upon their infringements of international copyright and upon slavery, only to find free speech denied him. He was offended by the familiarity of strangers and by the habits of those he met. No doubt he formed opinions hastily under the stress of public engagements, but he lived long enough to make the *amende honorable*. Dickens's impressions took literary form in *American Notes* (1842) and in *Martin Chuzzlewit* (1884) which ranks as one of his greatest achievements. *Martin Chuzzlewit* has a brilliant list of *dramatis personæ*, old Martin, Pecksniff, Jonas Chuzzlewit, Sarah Gamp, and Mark Tapley, and the requisite stage effects. But the plot and *dénouement* remain outrageously improbable. The Aristotelian doctrine that the end is the chief thing seems to have been the last to enter Dickens's mind, and the book remains great by reason of its triumphs in the realm of character, exclusively.

In 1844 Dickens started on his Italian tour, and before his return penned *Dombey* as far as little Paul's death, where it might fittingly have terminated. But the masterpiece was yet to come in *David Copperfield* (1850), which with *Martin Chuzzlewit* held the first place in Dickens's affections. Reminiscences of his childhood impart life to the opening sections, an early love-affair is idealized in Dora, while Mr. and Mrs. Micawber owe their being to Dickens's parents. The novel is rich in female portraiture—Betsy Trotwood, Dora, and Agnes

—and, in Uriah Heep, Dickens invented a new, though somewhat incredible, type of villain. The later novels from *Bleak House* (1853) to *Edwin Drood* show no advance in power, but afford rich illustration of Dickens's versatility in the sphere of the social and historical novel and the mystery tale. He also wrote three supreme examples of the Christmas story—the *Christmas Carol* (1843), the *Chimes* (1845), and the *Cricket on the Hearth* (1846).

With the exception, perhaps, of *Bleak House, A Tale of Two Cities*, and *Great Expectations*, Dickens's novels are loosely constructed. Events tend to be disconnected and to point to no conclusion. Even the characters fail to impart that unity of conception which is lacking in the plot : viewed under static conditions, they lack inherent motive power. With all this, Dickens seems to have held lofty views in regard to his art, and to have kept before himself definite ideals. He advanced, at any rate, from the string of adventures in *Pickwick* to the definite outline of *Bleak House*. With his keen eye for detail, Dickens possessed an essential part of the novelist's equipment, and no one has surpassed him in scenic presentation. He almost succeeds in endowing objects with life, and possessed no small share of the primitive animistic faculty. As Ruth Pinch in *Martin Chuzzlewit* passes the Temple, " merrily the fountain played, and merrily the dimples sparkled on its sunny face. Softly the whispering water broke and fell." No doubt, there is in this something of the " pathetic fallacy," but the account of the storm in the same book, and that of the waves sporting with the body of Quilp in the *Old Curiosity Shop*, constitute an artistic triumph :

It toyed and sported with its ghastly freight, now bruising it against the slimy piles, now hiding it in mud or long rank grass, now dragging it heavily over rough stones and gravel, now feigning to yield it to its own element, and in the same action luring it away, until, tired of the ugly plaything, it flung it on a swamp—a dismal place where pirates had swung in chains, through many a wintry night—and left it there to bleach.

At the same time Dickens has created a world of characters, the range of which is unsurpassed. Confining himself to particular types drawn from the lower middle class, he makes but occasional excursions elsewhere. It has been objected that his creations are recognizable only by some trick of gesture or expression, that his method is allied to Ben Jonson's. Dickens's fondness for acting explains, to some extent, his pose and effect, his effort to devise a situation, his love for melodrama. But this being granted, he has created in Sarah Gamp, Jonas Chuzzlewit, Fagin, Micawber, and the Wellers masterpieces of artistic portraiture. Squeers, indeed, exceeds the bounds of probability, but this is satiric portraiture, and Squeers is almost an institution. Inhuman though he be, he is no more so than Hugo's Quasimodo. Dickens's humour, where it is exclusively occupied with externals, tends, again, to the farcical and the grotesque, for example in Nadgett in *Martin Chuzzlewit*: " He was a short, dried-up, withered old man, who seemed to have secreted his very blood; for nobody would have given him credit for the possession of six ounces of it in his whole body. He was mildewed, threadbare, shabby; always had flue upon his legs and back; and kept his linen so secret by buttoning up and wrapping over, that he might have had none— perhaps he hadn't. He withdrew with another bow and without a word; opening the door no wider than was sufficient for his passage out and shutting it as carefully as before." But humour remains the very essence of Dickens, and Sarah Gamp is worthy to rank with Falstaff.

The following account of the discomfiture of Mr. Pecksniff, from *Martin Chuzzlewit*, is pure, unadulterated fun :

The young man had rather a long job in showing them out; for Mr. Pecksniff's delight in the tastefulness of the house was such that he could not help often stopping (particularly when they were near the parlour door) and giving it expression, in a loud voice and very learned terms. Indeed, he delivered, between the study and the hall, a familiar exposition of the whole science of architecture as applied to dwelling-houses, and was yet in the freshness of his eloquence when they reached the garden.

"If you look," said Mr. Pecksniff, backing from the steps, with his head on one side and his eyes half-shut that he might the better take in the proportions of the exterior: "If you look, my dears, at the cornice which supports the roof, and observe the airiness of its construction, especially where it sweeps the southern angle of the building, you will feel with me—— How do you do, sir? I hope you're well?"

Interrupting himself with these words, he very politely bowed to a middle-aged gentleman at an upper window, to whom he spoke: not because the gentleman could hear him (for he certainly could not) but as an appropriate accompanient to his salutation.

"I have no doubt, my dears," said Mr. Pecksniff, feigning to point out other beauties with his hand, "that this is the proprietor. I should be glad to know him. It might lead to something. Is he looking this way, Charity?"

"He is opening the window, pa!"

"Ha, ha!" cried Mr. Pecksniff softly. "All right! He has found I'm professional. He heard me inside just now, I have no doubt. Don't look! With regard to the fluted pillars in the portico, my dears——"

"Hallo!" cried the gentleman.

"Sir, your servant!" said Mr. Pecksniff, taking off his hat. "I am proud to make your acquaintance."

"Come off the grass, will you!" roared the gentleman.

"I beg your pardon, sir," said Mr. Pecksniff, doubtful of his having heard aright. "Did you——?"

"Come off the grass!" repeated the gentleman, warmly.

"We are unwilling to intrude, sir," Mr. Pecksniff smilingly began.

"But you are intruding," returned the other, "unwarrantably intruding. Trespassing. You see a gravel walk, don't you? What do you think it's meant for? Open the gate there! Show the party out!"

With that he clapped down the window again, and disappeared.

Mr. Pecksniff put on his hat, and walked with great deliberation and in profound silence to the fly, gazing at the clouds as he went, with great interest. After helping his daughters and Mrs. Todgers into that conveyance, he stood looking at it for some moments, as if he were not quite certain whether it was a carriage or a temple; but, having settled this point in his mind, he got into his place, spread his hands out on his knees, and smiled upon the three beholders.

Dickens's pathos reposes largely upon his efforts to keep in touch with his audience. Commanding an enormous popularity, he paid the debt by becoming the public's servant. The pathos of the death-scenes of Paul Dombey and little Nell appealed to this public, and served as an outlet for unexercised emotion. But this method of compelling tears leaves nothing to the imagination, and has little in common with Shakespeare or Webster, Dumas or Thackeray. Little Nell has been defended as " a child of romance " whose death is " purely symbolical," but this is to seek escape in allegory. Dickens's genuine pathos must be sought elsewhere, in the descriptions of the death of the Chancery prisoner in *Pickwick*, or the death of little Dorrit. As a stylist Dickens is often mannered, and his tendency to drop into metre remains a defect. But his zest for life imparts vigour to his work, and the narrative descriptions in *Pickwick* and *Copperfield* remain unsurpassed.

In almost every respect the work of Thackeray forms a contrast with that of Dickens, the explanation being found in the natural temperaments of the two men, partly in the conditions of their upbringing.

The literary ancestor of Thackeray was Fielding, whereas Dickens had most in common with Smollett. In the Preface to *Pendennis* Thackeray definitely links himself with the former, remarking that " since the author of *Tom Jones* was buried, no writer of fiction among us has been permitted to depict to his utmost power a man." It is characteristic of the method of the eighteenth century novelist that he constantly protrudes his head from behind the stage, in order to point out the merits or demerits of his creations. Thackeray is prone to the same trick : " Revenge may be wicked, but it's natural, I'm no angel," says Miss Rebecca Sharp in *Vanity Fair*, whereupon the novelist, thrusting up his head, ejaculates " And to say the truth, she certainly was not." The reader needs to be carefully reminded of the dramatic situation. " The argument stands thus," observes Thackeray in the early part of the same novel, " Osborne, in love with Amelia, has asked an old friend to dinner, and to Vauxhall—Jos. Sedley is in love with

Rebecca. Will he marry her? That is the subject now in hand." Again, he makes strenuous efforts to enlist our contempt in his description of Miss Crawley prostrate on her sick-bed :

> Picture to yourself, O fair young reader, a worldly, selfish, graceless, thankless, religionless old woman, writhing in pain and fear, and *without her wig*. Picture her to yourself, and ere you be old, learn to love and pray.

The introduction of the irrelevant detail "without her wig" imparts, as Professor Raleigh has shown, an altogether artificial quality to the satire. But Thackeray's method has its advantage, since it afforded the novelist opportunity for enforcing his teaching, whereas the objective method depends for its effect entirely upon sympathy. Thackeray is always ready to assist his readers' obtuseness, and his chapters sparkle with a profuse display of psychological detail :

> Mr. Joseph Sedley, luckily for his own peace, no more knew what was passing in his domestic's mind than the respected reader and I suspect what John or Mary, whose wages we pay, think of ourselves.

> Which of us is there can tell how much vanity lurks in our warmest regard for others, and how selfish our love is?

It is this wealth of psychological analysis, comparable with that of La Bruyère, that has laid Thackeray open to the charge of cynicism. No doubt he was over-sensitive to snobbery of all kinds, and from this only a humour such as Dickens possessed could have saved him : " Whenever shines the sun, you are sure to find folly basking in it. Knavery is the shadow at Folly's heels." His outlook on life was saddened by experience. His second child died in infancy, his wife fell into a mental decline four years after their marriage, and never recovered. Henceforth, Thackeray's philosophy may be summed up in the words, with which *Vanity Fair* closes : " Ah ! Vanitas Vanitatum ! which of us is happy in this world? Which of us has his desire? or, having it, is satisfied? Come, children, let us shut up the box and the puppets, for our play is played out." But this vivid sense of the immeasurable emotion pervading human life does not constitute cynicism. Thackeray pierces the trappings of his heroes, and sets his affection upon the simple-hearted. He has created no perfect characters; his sense of human frailty makes this impossible. Charlotte Brontë, a capable judge, maintained that "as usual Thackeray is unjust to women." He is as unsparing with women as with men, but the charge is just only to the extent that he failed to realize the highest character in women. In Helen Pendennis he had a rare opportunity, but ignored it. He drew fairer, though incomplete, portraits in Amelia Sedley and Ethel Newcome, but in Beatrix Esmond achieved his literary triumph.

Thackeray's pathos makes a special appeal to those who are unmoved by Dickens. His method approaches that of the great dramatists, and is characterized by restraint; it depends for its effect upon alliance with the imagination. The account of the death of Socrates in the *Phaedo* is not more moving than that of Colonel Newcome's last moments in the Grey Friars school, or the death of Samuel Titmarsh's child:

It has happened to me to forget the child's birthday, but to her never; and often in the midst of common talk comes something that shows she is thinking of the child still—some simple allusion that is to me inexpressibly affecting,

or the account of George Sedley's end:

No more firing was heard at Brussels—the pursuit rolled miles away. Darkness came down on the field and city; and Amelia was praying for George, who was lying on his face, dead, with a bullet through his heart.

Of style Thackeray was a past master, and, in this respect, superior to Scott no less than Dickens. He commanded a natural, elegant English, free from tortured brilliancies and over-ornateness. His literary method partook largely of improvisation. A voluminous writer, he worked without definite plan, composing novels *de longue haleine*, in which the sequence of events is conditioned from within. His books are thus dominated by their characters. If, as in *Pendennis*, Thackeray sketches a plan, he soon abandons it : he creates two or three characters and the story tells itself : " I do not control my characters. I am in their hands, and they take me where they please." In this respect he resembles Charlotte Brontë who wrote concerning *Villette* :

Most of the third volume is given to the development of the " crabbed Professor's " character. Lucy must not marry Dr. John; he is far too youthful, handsome, bright-spirited, and sweet-tempered; he is a " curled darling " of Nature and of Fortune, and must draw a prize in life's lottery. His wife must be young, rich, pretty; he must be made very happy indeed. If Lucy marries anybody, it must be the Professor—a man in whom there is much to forgive, much to " put up with." But I am not leniently disposed towards Miss *Frost* : from the beginning, I never meant to appoint her lines in pleasant places.

There is thus reason for Trollope's charge that Thackeray was unmethodical, though it is clear that a novelist who trusted to a strictly mechanical system was likely to lay particular stress on method. But Thackeray's interest in his characters remains intense ; he blubbers as freely as his most sensitive reader. Nor does he willingly let old friends go; many of the characters in *Pendennis* reappear in the *Newcomes*, while the *Newcomes* itself is supplemented by the *Virginians*. Thackeray's types are usually drawn from the upper classes—a characteristic in which he differs radically from Dickens. His interest in art and literature and his taste for a somewhat bohemian club-life tend to colour his pages. Pendennis, Clive Newcome, Warrington, and many another reflect aspects of Thackeray's own character, though Colonel Newcome is apparently adapted from life.

As a lecturer, Thackeray attained to a great reputation, though by different methods from Dickens. His lectures were essentially essays, delivered in a conversational style which never rose to the declamatory. His style produced its own effect without the adventitious aid of rhetoric, and his voice was attuned to the sonorities of the written matter. Dickens, on the other hand, was essentially a dramatic reader, acting the part of his characters and entering with intensity into the situation. The recital of Nancy's death in *Oliver Twist* is a case in point. "You have no idea," Dickens wrote to Forster, "how I have worked at the readings. I have tested all the serious passion in them by everything I know, made the humorous points more humorous; corrected my utterance of certain words; I learnt *Dombey* like the rest, and did it to myself often twice a day, with exactly the same pains as at night, over and over and over again." Compared with this vivid enunciation, Thackeray's academic method appears fastidious and even cold. Thackeray began to lecture in 1851, and had among his audience, at different times, Carlyle, Dickens, Macaulay, and Charlotte Brontë. In 1852 he set out for America to deliver a similar course. Much interest attaches to the subject-matter of his lectures on the *English Humourists of the Eighteenth Century*. As might be expected, in view of his obligations, Thackeray rated Fielding high, remarking on the constructive power, the minute observation, and varied characterization of *Tom Jones,* though he professed himself offended by the over-prominent tobacco-pouch and punch. Thackeray's air is somewhat jaunty; he constantly refers to the novelist as Harry, forgetting that he has to deal with a Justice of the Peace for Middlesex and Westminster, claimed as a descendant of the Counts of Hapsburg. Towards Steele he adopted much the same tone, and was severe with Swift and Sterne. He sermonizes over the author of *Gulliver,* finding his morals blasphemous. Swift's character is held up as a warning. Had you offended him, he would have "written a foul epigram about you, watched for you in a sewer and come out to assail you with a coward's blow and a dirty bludgeon." Sterne is represented as a jester rather than a humorist who lays down his carpet and tumbles on it within view of the audience. It is a relief to find that Thackeray recognized both humour and pathos in the scene with the ass in the seventh book of *Tristam Shandy*. But to Pope and Gay he was fairer; he notes the strain of tenderness and affection in Pope's character, and sums up Gay as " sleek, soft-handed and soft-hearted."

Thackeray's range was thus immense. A satirist, a writer of humorous verse, an artist, lecturer, and novelist, he has left us, in *Esmond*, what Pater considered the finest historical novel in the language.

INDEX